Ethosism

Ethosism

Self-Enslavement Abolitionist Manifesto

Jo M. Sekimonyo

RESOURCE *Publications* · Eugene, Oregon

ETHOSISM
Self-Enslavement Abolitionist Manifesto

Resource Publications
An Imprint of Wipf and Stock Publishers
199 W. 8th Ave., Suite 3
Eugene, OR 97401

www.wipfandstock.com

PAPERBACK ISBN: 978-1-7252-6534-9
HARDCOVER ISBN: 978-1-7252-6524-0
EBOOK ISBN: 978-1-7252-6525-7

11/13/20

Cogito, ergo dubito, ergo sum! (I think; therefore, I doubt, therefore I am!)

Contents

Roadmap | ix
Divorce Letter | xxvii
Preface | xxix
I Would Not Like | xxxi

Diagnostic: Sleeping Is Taunting Death | 1
1. What Is Love? | 3
2. Good Ol' Days | 10
3. Dumb and Dumber | 19
4. The Usual Suspects | 28

Veritas: Life Is the Leading Cause of Death | 37
5. Econometricks | 39
6. Unfinished Sentences | 50

Penitence!!! | 65
7. Tragic Love Story | 67
8. Echography of the Twenty-First Century | 82
Interview | 100

Nova Harmonia | 103
9. Tabula Rasa | 105
10. Alinéa | 117
11. Diamond Perfect Cut | 131

The Specter of Profit | 135

Bibliography | 137
Index | 141

Roadmap

"A map is not the territory it represents, but, if correct, it has a similar structure to the territory, which accounts for its usefulness."

—ALFRED HABDANK SKARBEK KORZYBSKI

Born: July 3, 1879, Warsaw, Poland
Died: March 1, 1950, Lakeville, Salisbury, CT

Divorce Letter

Shin Chae-ho

Born: November 7, 1880, Chungcheong, Sannaeri, Great Korean Empire

Died: February 21, 1936, Port Arthur, Empire of Japan

Quote: "The revolutionary path begins at destruction, thus opening up new ways for progress. However, revolution does not stop at destruction. There can be no destruction without construction; no construction without destruction . . . In the mind of the revolutionist, these two are indivisibly linked: destruction, ergo construction."

I Would Not Like

Franz Uri Boas

Born: July 9, 1858, Minden, Germany

Died: December 21, 1942, Columbia University Club of New York, New York, NY

Quote: "The passion for seeking the truth for truth's sake can be kept alive only if we continue to seek the truth for truth's sake."

What Is Love?

Anton Wilhelm Amo

Born: 1703, Axim, Ghana

Died: 1759, Ghana

Quote: "[. . .] it is the peculiarity of the human mind that it understands and acts through ideas, because it is very closely tied to the body."

Constantin Noica

Born: July 12, 1909, Vitănești

Died: December 4, 1987, Sibiu, Romania

Quote: "Eu sunt negustor de ideia."

Jacques Derrida

Born: July 15, 1930, El Biar, Algeria

Died: October 9, 2004, Paris, France

Quote: "Certain readers resented me when they could no longer recognize their territory, their institution."

Funmilayo Ransome-Kuti

Born: October 25, 1900, Abeokuta, Nigeria

Died: April 13, 1978, Lagos, Nigeria

Quote: "As for the charges against me, I am unconcerned. I am beyond their timid lying morality, and so I am beyond caring."

Good Ol' Days

Qiu Jin

Born: November 8, 1875, Shanyin County, Shuozhou, China

Died: July 15, 1907, Shanyin County, Shuozhou, China

Quote: "Autumn rain, autumn wind, they make one die of sorrow."

Cheikh Ahmadou Bamba (Khādimu 'r-Rasūl)

Born: 1853, Senegal

Died: July 19, 1927, Diourbel, Senegal

Quote: "I have received an order from my Lord to guide the people toward God, The Most High. Those who want to thread this path just have to follow me."

Max Simon Nordau

Born: July 29, 1849, Pest, Austria-Hungary

Died: January 23, 1923, Paris, France

Quote: "History is a melodrama on the theme of parasitism, characterized by scenes that are exciting or dull, as the case may be, and many a sudden stagetrick."

José Vasconcelos Calderón

Born: February 28, 1882, Oaxaca, Mexico

Died: June 30, 1959, Mexico City, Mexico

Quote: "Culture begets progress and without it cannot be required of people no moral conduct."

Dumb and Dumber

Theodor Wiesengrund Adorno

Born: September 11, 1903, Frankfurt, Germany

Died: August 6, 1969, Visp, Switzerland

Quote: "The almost insoluble task is to let neither the power of others, nor our own powerlessness, stupefy us."

Mustafa Kemal Atatürk

Born: May 19, 1881, Thessaloniki, Greece

Died: November 10, 1938, Dolmabahçe Palace, Istanbul, Turkey

Quote: "To write history is as important as to make history. If the writer does not remain true to the maker, then the unchanging truth takes on a quality that will confuse the humanity."

Negro Tom

Born: 1710, Benin

Died: 1790, United States of America

Quote: "No, Massa, it is best I had no learning, for many learned men be great fools."

Rosa Luxemburg

Born: March 5, 1871, Zamość, Congress Poland, Russian Empire

Died: January 15, 1919, Berlin, Germany

Quote: "Only to the rude ear of one who is quite indifferent does the song of a bird seem always the same."

The Usual Suspects

Ida Bell Wells-Barnett

Born: July 16, 1862, Holly Springs, MS

Died: March 25, 1931, Chicago, IL

Quote: "There must always be a remedy for wrong and injustice if we only know how to find it."

Saloth Sar

Born: May 19, 1925, Prek Sbauv, Cambodia

Died: April 15, 1998, Anlong Veng District, Cambodia

Quote: "I did not join the resistance movement to kill people, to kill the nation. Look at me now. Am I a savage person? My conscience is clear."

Federico del Sagrado Corazón de Jesús García Lorca

Born: June 5, 1898, Fuente Vaqueros, Spain

Died: August 18, 1936, Granada, Spain

Quote: "Death laid its eggs in the wound."

Naji Salim Hussain al-Ali

Born: 1938, Al-Shajara, Tiberias, Palestine

Died: August 29, 1987, London, United Kingdom

Quote: "The poor people are those who suffer, are sentenced to jail, and die without shedding tears."

Phoolan Devi

Born: August 10, 1963, Jalaun, India

Died: July 25, 2001, New Delhi, India

Quote: "I alone knew what I had suffered. I alone knew what it felt like to be alive but dead."

Econometricks

Gargi Vachaknavi

Born: 7th-century BCE, India

Died: 7th-century BCE, India

Quote: "The layer that is above the sky and below the earth, which is described as being situated between the earth and the sky and which is indicated as the symbol of the past, present, and future, where is that situated?"

Adolf Franz Karl Viktor Maria Loos

Born: December 10, 1870, Brno, Czech Republic

Died: August 23, 1933, Kalksburg. Austria

Quote: "The supporter of ornament believes that the urge for simplicity is equivalent to self-denial."

Frantz Omar Fanon

Born: July 20, 1925, Fort-de-France, Martinique

Died: December 6, 1961, Bethesda, MD, US

Quote: "Everything can be explained to the people, on the single condition that you really want them to understand."

Zera Yacob

Born: 1599, Aksum, Ethiopia

Died: 1602, Enfraz, Ethiopia

Quote: "If a liar, who desires to achieve wealth or honours among men, needs to use foul means to obtain them, he will say he is convinced this falsehood was for him a just thing. To those people who do not want to search, this action seems to be true, and they believe in the liar's strong faith."

Natsume Sōseki

Born: February 9, 1867, Ushigome, Tokyo, Japan

Died: December 9, 1916, Tokyo, Japan

Quote: "It is a shame that education just gives people the means to chop logic."

Unfinished Sentences

Olympe de Gouges

Born: May 7, 1748, Montauban, France

Died: November 3, 1793, Place de la Concorde, Paris, France

Quote: "You must fear the desperation of the poor and their subsequent revolts. It is always the rich who are attacked by their murderous hands, and often in their fury they make no distinction between the good and the bad."

Roadmap

John Kenneth Galbraith

Born: October 15, 1908, Iona Station, Ontario, Canada

Died: April 29, 2006, Cambridge, Massachusetts, US

Quote: "Under capitalism, man exploits man. Under communism, it's just the opposite."

Ong Boon Hua

Born: October 21, 1924, Sitiawan, Perak, Federated Malay States, British Malaya

Died: September 16, 2013, Bangkok, Thailand

Quote: "I don't think whether you believe in capitalism, or you believe in communism or socialism, I think nobody can dispute [it is right] to fight for a just and equal society."

Hin-mah-too-yah-lat-kekt, Hinmatóowyalahtq̓it

Born: March 3, 1840, Wallowa Valley, Oregon, United States

Died: September 21, 1904, Colville Indian Reservation, Washington, United States

Quote: "I am tired of talk that comes to nothing. It makes my heart sick when I remember all the good words and all the broken promises. There has been too much talking by men who had no right to talk."

Richard Nathaniel Wright

Born: September 4, 1908, Plantation, Roxie, Mississippi, U.S.

Died: November 28, 1960, Paris, France

Quote: "Make up your mind, Snail! You are half inside your house, And half-way out."

Magda Szabó

Born: October 5, 1917, Debrecen, Hungary

Died: November 19, 2007, Kerepes, Hungary

Quote: "Writing isn't an easy taskmaster. Sentences left unfinished never continue as well as they had begun. New ideas bend the main arch of the text, and it never again sits perfectly true."

Matsuo Chūemon Munefusa

Born: 1644, Near Ueno, Iga Province, Japan

Died: November 28, 1694, Osaka, Osaka Prefecture, Japan

Quote: "Do not seek to follow in the footsteps of the wise. Seek what they sought."

Penitence!!!

Cho Ki-chon

Born: November 6, 1913, Ael'tugeu, Vladivostok District, Russia

Died: July 31, 1951, Pyongyang, North Korea

Poem: Today you again smiled purely,
And said that you have overfilled the production plan threefold,
But I do not envy your achievement,
I can do even better,
But I like your smile.
Why is it so pure?

Tragic Love Story

Patrice Emery Lumumba

Born: July 2, 1925, Katakokombe, Democratic Republic of the Congo

Died: January 17, 1961, Lubumbashi, Democratic Republic of the Congo

Quote: "The aspirations of colonized and enslave peoples are everywhere the same; their lot too is the same."

George Washington Carver

Born: 1860s, Diamond, MO, US

Died: January 5, 1943, Tuskegee, AL, US

Quote: "Why something that build up human through commerce and trade is now destroying humanity?"

Jean-Paul Marat

Born: May 24, 1743, Boudry, Switzerland

Died: July 13, 1793, Paris, France

Quote: "It seems that the inevitable fate of man is never attain complete freedom: princes everywhere tend to despotism and the people to servitude."

Ali ibn Abi Talib

Born: Born: March 17, 599 AD, Mecca, Saudi Arabia

Died: January 29, 661 AD, Great Mosque of Kufa, Kufa, Iraq

Quote: "A poor man is like a foreigner in his own country."

Roadmap

Andrés de Jesús María y José Bello López

Born: November 29, 1781, Caracas, Venezuela

Died: October 15, 1865, Santiago, Chile

Quote: "By the corruption of language many other corruptions begin . . ."

Erich Kurt Mühsam

Born: April 6, 1878, Berlin, Germany

Died: July 10, 1934, Oranienburg concentration camp, Oranienburg, Germany

Quote: "The wage system is not altered in the slightest by the transferal of private capitalism to state capitalism, yet the wage system is the mark of exploitation."

George Ivanovich Gurdjieff

Born: January 13, 1866, Gyumri, Armenia

Died: October 29, 1949, Neuilly-sur-Seine, France

Quote: "If you want to lose your faith, make friends with a priest."

Lao She

Born: February 3, 1899, Beijing, China

Died: August 24, 1966, Beijing, China

Quote: "And so the result of several years of Everybody Shareskyism, other than slaughtering people, is for everybody to stand around and stare blankly at each other."

Echography of the Twenty-First Century

Aleksandr Ivanovich Herzen

Born: April 6, 1812, Moscow, Russia

Died: January 21, 1870, Paris, France

Quote: "Human development is a form of chronological unfairness, since late-comers are able to profit by the labors of their predecessors without paying the same price."

Ibn Battuta

Born: February 24, 1304, Tangier, Morocco

Died: 1377, Marrakesh, Morocco

Quote: "Who lives sees, but who travels sees more."

Herbert Alexander Simon

Born: Jun 15, 1916, Milwaukee, WI

Died: Feb 09, 2001, Pittsburgh, PA

Quote: "Everyone designs who devises courses of action aimed at changing existing situations into preferred ones."

Filiberto Ojeda Ríos

Born: April 26, 1933, in Naguabo, Puerto Rico

Died: September 23, 2005, Hormigueros, Puerto Rico

Quote: "They blame the people when the blame is on the system."

Dambudzo Marechera

Born: June 4, 1952, Rusape, Zimbabwe

Died: August 18, 1987, Harare, Zimbabwe

Quote: "The old man died beneath the wheels of the twentieth-century. There was nothing left but stains, bloodstains, and fragments of flesh . . . And the same thing is happening to my generation."

Kozo Uno

Born: November 12, 1897, Kurashiki, Okayama Prefecture, Japan

Died: November 12, 1897, Kurashiki, Okayama Prefecture, Japan

Quote: "The commodity originally appears upon becoming the property of some person."

José Julián Martí Pérez

Born: January 28, 1853, Havana, Cuba

Died: May 19, 1895, Cuba

Quote: "Today we are experiencing the notion of influencer and influenced."

Edward Bellamy

Born: March 26, 1850, Chicopee, MA

Died: May 22, 1898, Chicopee, MA

Quote: "Looking Backward was written in the belief that the Golden Age lies before us and not behind us."

Nova Harmonia

Mohammad Abdus Salam

Born: January 29, 1926, Punjab, Pakistan

Died: November 21, 1996, Oxford, United Kingdom

Quote: "From time immemorial, man has desired to comprehend the complexity of nature in terms of as few elementary concepts as possible."

Alinéa

Joseph Auguste Anténor Firmin

Born: October 18, 1850, Cap-Haïtien, Haiti

Died: September 19, 1911, Saint Thomas, United States Virgin Islands

Quote: "All men are endowed with the same qualities and the same faults, without distinction of color or anatomical form. The races are equal."

Lu Xun

Born: September 25, 1881, Shaoxing, China

Died: October 19, 1936, Shanghai, China

Quote: "Hope is like a path in the countryside. Originally, there is nothing— but as people walk this way again and again, a path appears."

Boris Leonidovich Pasternak

Born: February 10, 1890, Moscow, Russia

Died: May 30, 1960, Boris Pasternak's House Museum, Peredelkino, Russia

Quote: "When a great moment knocks on the door of your life, it is often no louder than the beating of your heart, and it is very easy to miss it."

Roadmap

Fumiko Kaneko

Born   January 25, 1903, Yokohama, Kanagawa, Japan

Died   July 23, 1926, Utsunomiya, Tochigi, Japan

Quote: "Living is not synonymous with merely having movement. It is moving in accordance with one's will . . . one could say that with deeds, one begins to really live. Accordingly, when one moves by means of one's own will and this leads to the destruction of one's body, this is not a negation of life. It is an affirmation."

Robert Beck

Born: August 4, 1918, Chicago, IL, US

Died: April 28, 1992, Culver City, CA, US

Quote: "An emotional debt is hard to square."

Arthur Schopenhauer

Born: February 22, 1788, Gdańsk, Poland

Died: September 21, 1860, Frankfurt, Germany

Quote: "The alchemists in their search for gold discovered many other things of greater value."

Gaston Bachelard

Born: June 27, 1884, Bar-sur-Aube, France

Died: October 16, 1962, Paris, France

Quote: "There is no original truth, only original error."

Tabula Rasa

Simón José Antonio de la Santísima Trinidad de Bolívar y Palacios

Born: July 24, 1783, Caracas, Venezuela

Died: December 17, 1830, Santa Marta, Colombia

Quote: "To do something right it must be done twice. The first time instructs the second."

Pyotr Alexeevich Kropotkin

Born: December 9, 1842, Moscow, Russia

Died: February 8, 1921, Dmitrov, Russia

Quote: "Competition is the law of the jungle, but cooperation is the law of civilization."

Abu Hamid Al-Ghazali

Born: 1058, Tous, Iran

Died: December 19, 1111, Tous, Iran

Quote: "Never have I dealt with anything more difficult than my own soul, which sometimes helps me and sometimes opposes me."

Alfred Russel Wallace

Born: January 8, 1823, United Kingdom of Great Britain and Ireland

Died: November 7, 1913, Broadstone, Dorset, United Kingdom

Quote: "Truth is born into this world only with pangs and tribulations, and every fresh truth is received unwillingly."

Henri Marie Coandă

Born: June 7, 1886, Bucharest, Romania

Died: November 25, 1972, Bucharest, Romania

Quote: "In my opinion, we should search for a completely different flying machine, based on other flying principles."

Gertrude Elizabeth Margaret Anscombe FBA

Born: March 18, 1919, Limerick, Ireland

Died: January 5, 2001, Cambridge, United Kingdom

Quote: "An intentional object is given by a word or a phrase which gives a description under which."

Sojourner Truth

Born: Rifton, NY

Died: November 26, 1883, Battle Creek, MI

Quote: "Then I will speak to the ashes."

Diamond Perfect Cut

Piero Sraffa

Born: August 5, 1898, Turin, Italy

Died: September 3, 1983, Cambridge, United Kingdom

Quote: "In economic theory, the conclusions are sometimes less interesting than the routes by which they are reached."

Jean-Michel Basquiat

Born: December 22, 1960, Brooklyn, New York, NY

Died: August 12, 1988, Great Jones Street, New York, NY

Quote: "I start a picture and I finish it."

The Specter of Profit

Sarah Moore Grimké

Born: November 26, 1792, Charleston, SC

Died: December 23, 1873, Hyde Park, Boston, MA

Quote: "I ask no favors for my sex. I surrender not our claim to equality. All I
ask of our brethren is, that they will take their feet from off our necks,
and permit us to stand upright on that ground which God designed
us to occupy."

Divorce Letter

"The revolutionary path begins at destruction, thus opening up new ways for
progress. However, revolution does not stop at destruction.
There can be no destruction without construction; no construction
without destruction . . . In the mind of the revolutionist, these two
are indivisibly linked: destruction, ergo construction."

—SHIN CHAE-HO

I AM SO NERVOUS while I am writing this letter. The unconscious nature of
self-deception can fog our dreams at our own peril. I don't know or understand why you became part of my identity or why villains and saints in my
family adore you. When you were an adolescent, I pretended to enjoy your
physical abuses and insults. At times, our bond felt like the best thing that
had ever happened to me. I have come to the realization that my thoughts
and feelings were not accurate reflections of reality.

Lately, everything feels wrong. Reliving our memories has become
something painful. Karl Marx, the drunken racist hobo who used to piss
on our street, warned me about you; however, it was too soon, too late. You
obviously only care about yourself. Even after countless therapy sessions
with John Kenneth Galbraith and Rudolf Alfred Meidner, you fail to figure
out why you treat the people, whom you claim to have nothing but affection
for, the way you do. Two centuries later, I still burst into tears every night,
still too afraid of letting go and being alone, but I have learned the hard way
not to have permanent sentiment for temporary emotions.

During the most recent global commerce and trade debacles, I re-
alized that you will never mature. You will never stop. I cannot stay in a

relationship where there is no mutual admiration or consideration; I have decided to give myself the opportunity to live. I might not have the right key to open a new door, but keys are useless when it comes to cracking open dreams.

It is not easy to tell you this, I recently began spending some time with somebody from work. Because you are still in my life, I feel anxious, angry, or scared when I am with a new mate, but it is not fair for me to pretend that our relationship is going to work. There is something between you and I that I can no longer pretend doesn't exist: repugnance. My leaving is the best thing for everyone involved.

Letting out all the garbage stored inside of my brain was a cathartic exercise. I know in my heart that I will forever hate you. I shall always remember our time together as the worst time in my life.

Please don't call me. Don't text me. Don't even mutter my name.

Go to hell,
Sane Human

Note to self: remember to post this letter tomorrow.

Preface

ANY DISCUSSION ABOUT ETHOS, from which the word ethics is part and parcel of the same tree, must include the notion of morality. In a political economic context, there is an absolute morality to the behavior of all economies within every society.

Societies grew out of isolated villages, which in turn grew out of isolated clan and tribes, which in turn grew from family groupings. No member of a family would long remain a member of said family group for long if they stole from their children, sibling, parents, or another family group member. They would be cast out at best, or stoned to death.

To steal was in any primitive society almost above any other crime except murder, the paramount sin of society. Today the rich enjoy a watered-down version of such extreme cures to such crimes. They usually cost society in more ways than one, and thus steal not only from an individual or individuals, but also from the society as a whole, to sustain their lavish lifestyle. The poor are locked up for a determined amount of time at a cost to society far greater, in most instances, than the amount which they stole.

All societies are based on a particular set of common understandings; rules of law which the adherents subscribe to. We juggle with the variations of words like socialism, communism, capitalism, Marxism, free markets, democracy, and even libertarianism for whatever purpose makes us happy. Let us here be clear: no human should be at an advantage, or disadvantage, in the protection of their social rights, commerce and trade liberty, and political freedoms. In Latin, it can be said in one word: Aequitas, meaning equity, justice, evenness, uniformity, fair play, and impartiality. We would say, in English, equality.

I Would Not Like

"The passion for seeking the truth for truth's sake can be kept alive
only if we continue to seek the truth for truth's sake."

—FRANZ URI BOAS

A GREEK SAGE WAS said to have been projected in Yevgeny Yevtushenko's
fear-provoking encomium, I would like, a picturesque contempt of our entitlement, by my previous Missio Dei. Yevgeny simultaneously yearned to
be someone other than himself: perchance, Publius Terentius Afer and Jean
Maximilien Lamarque, at the same time. His work displayed a blending of
pain and traditional joy that broke practical judgment boundaries.

Who is Jo M. Sekimonyo? Congolese roots, American fermented,
globally bottled, a pleasure and agony canvasser, and an ideological mambi
(nonconformist); a machetero deliberately confronted by corybantic circumstances of existing.

"I write what I like," said Steve Biko. I write what I deeply hate.
Somehow, we both denounce the same crap: socioeconomic injustice. My
long-winded pieces might one day intersect with numerous petitions from
other mutineers to form streams and lakes of insurgency. I spill my verity
and discordance not to enrapture an audience, but to summon contemporaneous probity, and to add my voice to clamoring crowds disrelishing
modern-day social and political economy constructs. I no longer pore over
contemporary literature like I did when I was innocent. I could care less
about echoing or reciting past and present hopes or nightmares. I now continually tune my acuities by living. Yes, it is an awful cerebral diet; however,
it's pertinent to discern plausibility with certainty.

I coldly abstain from being everyone else. I pride myself on having a rhinoceros-tough skin which safeguards me against the usual flapdoodle. I am fiercely opinionated and allergic to poorly patched arguments, and I am often at odds with both the social order and deities around me. Like a poltergeist, I delight in wreaking havoc on psychological and cerebral closed-mindedness just as I would any other form of fanaticism or fallacy. I grind my teeth to the mudslinging between Marcus Mosiah Garvey, Jr. and William Edward Burghardt Du Bois; still, I wouldn't betray either of them to put $300 in my pocket.

Diagnostic

Sleeping Is Taunting Death

1

What Is Love?

"[...] it is the peculiarity of the human mind that it understands
and acts through ideas, because it is very closely tied to the body."
—ANTON WILHELM AMO

IN THE SPIRIT OF full disclosure, I ought to make a clean breast of my
gloomiest aberration. I once paid (not got paid) in rubies to slog on a rust-
ing pirate vessel as an apprentice. The gig didn't last long; my lack of submissiveness was not suited for the voyage. As the crew chased after me with
a noose, I jumped off the ship and swam across the deep sea. I later learned
the fate of those lured tyros who were left behind. The boat sailed to a minuscule, obscure island where these sycophants were scholastically battered
and sodomized until they turned into ideological zombies. Then, before
sunrise, they were immolated at the shrine of the island's sacred gods: Karl
Marx, Alfred Marshall, Friedrich Hayek, and John Maynard Keynes; and
for the negroes, Sir William Arthur Lewis. Such horrendous proselytism
unquestionably turns a sympathetic Mu'mina into a wicked oppressor or a
vicious predator, culminating the cyclic inferno.

As luck would have it, once I reached dry land, my saneness and ve-
racity did not make my life easier. I was hunted down like a witch by mobs
of sophists and anarchists. They sought to castrate and then burn me on
a cross for my public plea to get rid of capitalism and my enmity for socialism and communism. I have come to expect that even people whose

3

beliefs differ from strict economic orthodox views and Islamic economics shenanigans will find my voice to be exceedingly radical, but heresy?

At times, they stunned me with makeshift projectiles filled with bullshit. I would have been composing sonnets to Mehdi Ben Barka with a silent pen right now had I failed to regain consciousness and had been caught. Instead, I add my voice to the clamoring crowds who oppose modern-day social and political economy constructs.

Sadly, my frustrating entanglements do elevate my reasoning to consciousness-piercing decibels. It pains me to admit that my sermon against the prevailing social, commerce and trade, and political bonds inherited from the eighteenth-century factories, invasions, and travesties passes for a strange sound instead of an alarming siren.

Ideals have proven to be the only way to exist. Without picking up a pen and writing them down, you desist to exist. It is so refreshing, then, when someone happens to relish the rhythm of my composition and can distinguish a signal from the noise. I am expressing gratitude with joy and humility to the one percenter who have decrypted my wrath and made sense of my rants to the lagging 99-percenters. You have added your voices to mine, and suddenly people are noticing!

"Eu sunt degustar de ideia." (I am the merchant of an idea.)

—CONSTANTIN NOICA

If you rode the previous roller coaster of Economic Jihad, my call for ending antiquated social axioms defining us, you have been exposed to the awful rumpus going on in my head. No matter how much I try, I just cannot bring myself to accept intolerance or prejudice in life. I am all for the death penalty when it comes to punishing dummies and hypocrites who brandish their intellectual sheriff badges to aid and abet socioeconomic genocide. Their presence makes my fingers and toes tingle with ire. I feel compelled to either choke them or emotionally jet away.

What is there to learn from my first literary crusade? Communism was an experiment of Frankensteinien proportions. It was thrown out when the importance of human beings integrated the notion of the rational and gained grounds in most part of the red world.

A minuscule number of cynical rich kids and former cold war mécènes have yet to come to terms with the factual evidence of communism's inherent sins. Dazed by the twenty-first century's range and depth of social and political time warp, these pathetic coalitions indict the obsessional

4

neoliberal agenda polluting transnational policy and third world gushes. They inaudibly vindicate the disillusioned Cuban and Vietnamese elite. With the same stomach-churning candor, they discount North Korea's sociopathic regime and its sadistic, mammoth-sized penitentiary camps.

On the same pyramid of foolishness, I list socialist caricatures who would cite France as a success story. That blinkered nation's socialist façade persists with the help of the western nations' joint ownership and abuses of their "former" colonies. Furthermore, France's anti-immigrant policies confirm that its socialism is merely a parody. As far as the current Middle East social retch, I reserve the right to demystify Islamic economics for reasons you, the reader, will come to disentangle.

What is there to say about the rest of the world, which is terrified of shrieks that excavate skepticism over modern prime commerce and trade contrivances and expand the possibility of a new road? Swimming against the stream is a lonesome voyage.

So, let me say it plainly: the canonization of capitalism is without merit. The Victorian's scheme that has made humiliation a quotidian routine for most common mortals is now tilting the globe to the brink of collapse. Yet, no sane mind or credible creature has shown up to push for its eviction from our streams of consciousness.

Economists' schemes are rife with outdated axioms masquerading as common sense that should elicit only one response: rejection. Deplorably, most of their half-baked concepts are based on observations of creatures who only exist in economists' fantasies, yet, they continue to be unchallenged. Their rulings are used to launch precarious policies that devastate the prospect of a dignified existence for billions of people on this dying planet.

Scratch the surface of bellicose intellectual eunuchs and the one-track mind of the mutineers' masquerade, and you will figure out on your own that their treatises are merely an exercise to paint pervasive social class disparities in beautiful charts and convoluted patterns. Most of the trendy economic tunes are nothing more than hoopla for chic serfdom (or should I use the proper terminology, here: the self-enslaved's empowerment).

Alas, the public has mistaken these philosophical pieces of academic aerobics for condemnations of global social, commerce and trade, and political injustices. As a result, every Tom, Dick, Harry, and Henriette absurdly has faith in capitalism and naïvely believes that he or she is one little step away from the gaining side of inclusive socioeconomic injustice.

Proper implantation of "better trading conditions" or "sustainability" adds to a peppy slogan a *certain je ne sais quoi* that chokes out rancorous debates on socio-politico-economic injustice and gets me pumped up for at least two seconds. Suddenly, grim realities sneak into the scene and ruin my optimism with gradually deepening despondency. I cannot help but be disgusted every time the public galvanizes with fury and thunder behind petty structural adjustment ultimatums (i.e. standard working hours or minimum wage).

Socioeconomic inequality is an ambiguous theme exasperating radical movements for a change of humankind's moral compass. Two very distinct elements of inequality—disparity and injustice—are squeezed under one huge umbrella. A socioeconomic disparity is an inherent imperfection of any society and requires structural changes to balance it out. Injustice of any kind is a deliberate discriminatory social construct and demands social repentance and mending to get rid of the evil.

To put these two conversations, disparity and injustice, in a cut-and-dried analogy: class disparity is to socio-politico-economic injustice what civil rights are to the abomination of slavery. The lack of a clear moral line in the sand between underlying social conditions and systematic inhumanity blurs the real essence of political economy examinations which have become a prerequisite to weighing civil rights.

> "Certain readers resented me when they could
> no longer recognize their territory, their institution."
>
> —JACQUES DERRIDA

When you write a book to be slowly digested, not a gimmick or a sales pitch, you have to embrace your imperfections and accept insolence. It was once suggested that no sane mind would want to touch my scathing philippic. A fisherman who whispered in my ear that only one percent of the river is useful to him hardened my impenitence.

If you happen to be one of the fuming readers (and a passionately sluggish creature, to top it off) who wonders what the hell Ethosism is, well, I am confident that by the end of this book, you will not be able to lecture a room full of agnostic capitalists or redirect the remaining Marxist lambs away from the cliff of promise. It will take you more than one slow ride on this roller coaster.

If you are expecting to read The Arthashastra of the twenty-first century, well, you are in for a monumental disappointment. I have never felt particularly pretentious; I am compelled by bibliophiles' sluggishness to highlight the fact that my antidote for the current global socio-politico-economic evenhandedness departs from the highly toxic slogans of political economy's coquettes. This book relies on the certainty that we become color, gender, shape, size, and class-blind when we have a motive to reduce to ashes our global community's sordid conventions.

A piece of art is a *coup d'essai* to crank up sentiment in people. It can be full of characters that elicit different emotions when observed from different distances. Unlike any other form of expression, an essayist gives readers the full right and responsibility to add to a crafted sentence a voice, a décor, and a heartbeat that they see as a best fit. An initiator of vibrations is forever held hostage in strangers and comrades' brains, who indiscreetly stab or attempt to deface the only thing left to a writer: a thought.

I bare my back to the vain, the agony, and the delight that exists on different parts of the globe. Afterward, I sequester my mind to decipher the sensation. Though I lack digital dexterity to skillfully play any instrument, my words are my music. I compose the score; it is up to your bravura and audacity to reach for the instrument of your choice and serenade the rest of the world.

To a painter, the ultimate compliment is a tear. As a hostile writer, I am in the business of making readers disgusted with contemporary social constructs and contracts. I will not falsify my melancholia with Nina Simone's lamentation, "Please don't let me be misunderstood." I will not allow Maecenas and traducers to hunt and squash me like Leon Trotsky, like a rat. Any attempt to puncture my conscience and free Alfred Willi or Rudi Dutschke will be vain. I plead for 33 strips of flesh to be torn from my chest, then shekkeh me as I go west and cross the River Styx to soul kiss M'Balia Camara.

This book contains two successive waves of thoughts. At times, I encapsulate years' worth of intrusion into one phrase; while at other times, a second of awareness births out a multitude of pages. Be warned, however: I would not rest in peace until my brain is served as a feast to five Korowai tribe children, five years of age, sitting on piles of Carolyn Bryant Donham and Truganini statuettes, staring at Giangiacomo Feltrinelli portrait while they are being serenaded by a blind Danish comedian singing "Con Te Partiro." Five days later, the ashes of my remains and the leftovers from the banquet should be spewed around Cateura, Paraguay.

"As for the charges against me, I am unconcerned. I am beyond their timid lying morality, and so I am beyond caring."

—FUNMILAYO RANSOME-KUTI

Here, you have bravely embarked on a death-defying journey into my hunch. Ethosism is partly a dedication to Anton Wilhelm Amo, a victim of academia's bigotry and his own scholastic queerness, which made him pay the ultimate price: deprivation of relevance. At this moment, I take great pleasure in making Isaac Newton roll in his tomb by causing you to read the name of an ingenious philosopher, Robert Hooke. In doing so, you are saving my integrity.

To show my gratitude of your acceptance or inquisitiveness, I am going to bang devilishly on your thick, disenchanted walls until you are awakened and ready to help me chase away the reckless demons residing in every ordinary mortal; to raise Cain.

I could have easily opted for a smoother route on this journey by charmingly reciting stony theories that frame the main current social and political ideologies. But I refuse to abstain from abusing my right of conscience. To abandon any of my infuriating traits and diffuse my identity is not unbearable; it is unthinkable. As a shameless dissenter, I live with the urge of finishing brave protagonists' sentences or ruining conformists' contentment.

My advice to you and anyone with a handful of neurons that respond to empathetic stimuli, who have been bitten by a serpent with dollar signs at the end of its tail, is: Don't run around like a chicken with its head cut off. Keep reading this torturous book: it is an emetic to rid your conscience of lies. For the sake of humanity, everyone should be mortified to die without winning some victory over pervasive absurdities.

This literary ayahuasca-fueled experience will inundate your nerves with Thomas Clarkson's apparition. The attempt to take a chunky bite of capitalism, communism, or socialism's reshuffled stances and spit it into a blazing fire is not made in vain. There is no better time than the twenty-first century to shift the ground of the global inequality dispute by zooming in on socioeconomic injustice.

What can you and I positively achieve? Fight cynicism. Urgency and persistence are of the essence. We are well equipped to stamp out wealth distribution debauchery and pave the way for an alternative to the Victorian's exoneration of injustices. Through the pain, always remember that nobody comes from nowhere. There is a story behind everybody. The same goes for ideas: none come from thin air. A question precedes every answer—or, at least, one should. Courage is indubitably the most glorified of all virtues, while for a creature like myself, encouragement is most arousing of all vices. In life, nothing is worth more than paying attention.

2

Good Ol' Days

"Autumn rain, autumn wind, they make one die of sorrow."

—QIU JIN

IN EVERY AGE AND part of the world, we hear these doleful jeremiads, "life was simpler and great in those days." For hark-backers to joyously appreciate the geometric functions used to evaluate man, bird, and beast, the narratives of the past have to enrich the current junctures of humanity's plot development. The antiquity accounts are brilliant minds' expressions on subjects of the deepest moment, full of vehement misapprehensions. Oratorical pageantry may be trapped in historians' ears and jotted down on a wall with an injection of wanting. For religious institutions and monarchs, the mass printing, the critical treatment of testimonies, and the ways and means of ferreting out phonies are the human race's original sins.

I rolled the history dice eleven times, and nature plugged in humor, mother nature kneeled on one knee, and Europe uninterruptedly came face up, each time. It could be the result of cosmic interference in my thought process, or the cauldron of repressed anger spilling over. The panorama of humans' chronicles makes Europe a glaring starting point for exposing centric biases. Europeans embellished folklore, and folkways are nowadays envied and venerated by the whole world.

There was a time when this large area of land between Asia and the Atlantic Ocean's quirks were part savage and part doltish. Live subjects were dismembered to investigate human body function. Malodor was believed to cause chlamydia. Quacks gained opulence and favors by alleging to have a tacit understanding and a mastery of supernatural phenomenon. European men had magic spells down pat to induce prurient thoughts in their prospective mates. A man abducted, defiled, and molested whom he surmised to be the light of his life until she gave credence to his phantasm and conceded to become his. This was the conventional means of tying the knot. A mother's previous mates were believed to pass on their features to her children by means other than insemination. Ignoramuses were immaculate creatures. Fortune telling by facial deformities was considered an exact science. Inhumanness was a magnanimous gesture and a superlative. Citizens accused migrants of bringing in diseases and crime. The public spectacle of tearing a human being from limb from limb was a sour-sweet delight.

In all fairness, the period of time when an empire or civilization ascendancy was at its height, its mores sunk to the lowest point of degradation, is a habitual coincidence. Every civilization has its peculiar moral decay. Mesopotamian brides were ordered to have sex with random strangers before their husbands touched the goods. There were no exceptions on the inequity that Egyptians, Aztecs, and the Zhou practiced upon the poor and the defeated. In Zhong Guo, heinous torture recipes were celebrated, and 'Killing the Chickens to Shock The Monkey' was a common tactic. Persians went as far to castrate their enemies' sons, while the Iroquois simply erased the Neutral Confederacy from existence. Every public festivity of fierce battle triumph archetypally included the mass raping of vanquished wives and daughters. The Māori had a different approach: they caged the conquered women and children at the beach to die in great pain, and ate the men.

Few moral turpitudes transcended with the same pretext and perversity as the oldest social arrangement and asymmetrical division of labor, slavery. To a large extent, slavery was woven into the fabric of empires' wealth and societies' psychosis alike. Humans captured others for every deplorable reason one can imagine: atrocious extravaganza, forced labor, or commodities. The Vikings cruised off the English coasts for easy pickings. The Oyo kingdom refined cavalry assault to capture slaves swiftly and well. Everywhere under the sun, the children of slaves were to become nothing more than slaves. For the most part, slaves were domestic servants. However, communities did not sharpen their hunting humans' skills solely to make their lives easier. Some abductees met a brutal end to indulge bloodthirsty gods.

Diabolically, every nation demonstrated an awareness of investment ricocheting on productivity and increasing employment. Confucius fought vehemently to preserve the Chinese slavery institution as it was dwindling away.

Slavery was not color shade based, until late in the game. African villains like King Diogo I Nkumbi a Mpudi[1] unbolted the spirit of the Africanization of slave trades. The Sultanate of Oman played an essential part of blackening this sinister trade. Their acts ultimately lead to the extinction of the notion that blacks were humans. The conquistadores' appetite and passion for slave trading was a beast of another kind. To evade bias succinctness and to increase comprehension, I shall say that many Spaniard sages objected the use of the disingenuous terminology trade. Nonetheless, they felt no compunction when Europeans purchased Africans caged and sold by other Africans, or a child hawked by its parents.

The sheer variation of lunacy in history indicates the universality of the moron outbreak and its spread. In every corner of the world, intimidators and sociopaths were vividly admired. Given the opportunity to decide who shall dictate social order, old societies invariably chose absolute psychopaths. Masochism's appeal made the most merciless creatures into rulers, sages, and prophets. Casting doubt on the awareness of enlightened philosophers or highlighting the provincialism in their literary works is not without plenty of merits. Kindness and remorse as a potentate's primary attributes were not part of a serious dialogue.

There was no difference in inhumaneness's standards around the world. Essayists related events in which they took part by embroidering the truth and coincidences. The oppressors and the oppressed saw classlessness as an absurd social ideal. If one country had more gold than another, it was inevitably better off, or got beat up and its gold sacked by a bully empire. The best route to national prosperity was accumulating slaves and gold and silver ingots. From this angle, all of our ancestors appear to be downright greedy and sadistic.

> "I have received an order from my Lord to guide the people toward God, The Most High. Those who want to thread this path just have to follow me."
>
> —CHEIKH AHMADOU BAMBA

1. Heywood, "Slavery and its transformation in the kingdom of Kongo: 1491–1800.",1–22.

Good Ol' Days

Anicius Manlius Severinus Boëthius wondered: "If there is a God, whence proceed so many evils? If there is no God, whence cometh any good?"[2] If gold is the root of all evil, is it the ideal pretext for an impecunious right to commit evil deeds? Theism should be compelled to have a great rational foundation of its sacred values than anything else. Poltroon sanctimonious talk about becoming abruptly omniscient. Their logic for communities' vital subjugation to an omnipotent creature was mired in tomfoolery from its inception. Mortals were not cognizant that prudence was not a subject of convoluted competence which required it to be exhibited in the subtlety of matters. Warmongering empires and brutal groups pummeled and enslaved communities accused of being morally degenerated. This view was more than a belief; it was a mandate from heaven. If you committed atrocities in order to win a battle, then God must be on your side, and he wanted it that way: a perfect victor's logic.

Sermons driven in fiery sleet words and images enchanted all who heard it. The flaming life of the moment and the extempore discourses orated during a deluge or abnormal disaster was echoed by priests and charlatans using the same dramatic tone, to hypnotize the naïve packs. The voice of doom's potency was in words of good and evil chemistry. Typical theologies' points of departure marked new divine frontlines and reshuffled the characterization of saints and fools. Within a religious parcel, ideological purity was at all times at the center of its effort. The mass was told where wise loyalty should lie; holy orders went beyond rechristening the contending parties. You were denounced as an atheist if you expressed a reservation about the credibility of old scriptures. It was impossible to escape senile religious dogmas which led one to magnify the merits of deities.

Plausible reasons justified theology's powerful influence over dialectical ingenuity. The science of medicine would be useless among people free from disease. Religion, like a satire, was fed by inflating the natural flaws and misfortunes of society. Long periods of prosperity were its whirlwind. When society was in upheaval, it shone forth with supreme splendor. The desperation for escaping from real time and space, the threat of apocalyptic fury, and fear of the ambiguous paranormal smothered native wit. In a Shangri-La free from crimes, commotions, and disturbances, there was still prophets and divinities. Theism encompassed the realm of space and the horizon of learning.

---

2. Boethius, "The consolation of philosophy (VE Watts, Trans.).", 124.

The development of towns and the expansion of commerce disrupted seductive paganism. Verdicts on the nonphysical mechanic of humans' existence asserted the primacy of their idiosyncratic interpretation of a Maker or Makers, and paranormal signals. There was no moderation in religion's raison d'être and preposterous proclamations. Words were blameworthy as a medium to transmit the god-mandated bloodbaths. Commitment to the insane and cynical explanation of the gods' hints demanded outright self-deception or a lack of humor. Mockery of their harebrained guidebooks, or dissent, was not tolerated. Spiritual cartels hypnotized peasants at will and replaced obstreperous rulers with blue-blooded acquiescent lackeys.

Theology saturated the atmosphere of the ol' days. Humankind accepted forgeries and legends with childlike faith. The search for natural causation was impertinent. Sterile criticism of historical works had the same amateurism as medical practices. Religious factions did at times incorporate anodyne stances favorable to a balanced view of controversial questions. For the most part, only those who attained the stipulated degree of purity would be spared of afterlife torment, was their driving theological imperative. An equally unmeasured claim of "God is on my side" aided and abetted brutes in their rationalization for demeaning their enemies through decapitation, disembowelment, incineration, and other creative inhuman ways. Just as with any dominant segment of the ancient way of life, religious institutions relied on violence and coercion for its existence.

> "History is a melodrama on the theme of parasitism,
> characterized by scenes that are exciting or dull,
> as the case may be, and many a sudden stagetrick."
>
> —MAX SIMON NORDAU

Portraiture, or a Vedic chant trap, is a posture, a voice, and gesticulations that may be lost forever if the expression of intent is not well looked after. The strain of hominids' apathy dwarfs coherent anxiety. Waking up with a mouth full of tiny fingers, we worry more about our demise than the pain we inflict. A science which can't achieve its appropriate function is well deserving of being written off as a pseudoscience. The unpalatable truth was the lack of a litmus test specific to social and political answers and ripostes exacerbating the world. Humankind's appetite for agonizing others and the disjointing pure act of altruism is as old as life itself.

Weakling scholars found happiness in their orthodox cerebral routines and themes. Early idealists sought to wipe out a principal of imperfection what was thought to be human nature. Audacious study stimulated the character and fortunes of nations, and was aimed at derailing acedia. Barthélemy de Laffemas's treatises urging the prosperous French to care for the poor have survived harsh censors and denunciations. Around the same epoch, the philosophical dimensions of social and political reform ideas were also sought after, elsewhere. Shaihu Usman dan Fodio's bold condemnations of peasants' treatments by abominable rulers altered a sub-continent. In summoning the rich conscience or killing despots, they reeled naïve souls into great fables.

Conflicts between and within métiers are also as old as life itself. While all the world was changing around the eighteenth-century, the brawl of manufactured zealots and agriculture's aficionados was over Europe's mighty rulers' positive discrimination and philosophical commitment. In the midst of the raging philosophical battle, moral sentiments of exorcising injustice were no more or less neglected. Until the doctrine of science was enunciated, no fair verdict was possible. To Adam Smith, the political economy is a device for politicians to care of the public or to assist individuals in enriching themselves. Stuart Mill later appended the proposition. The blunt truth shook western congregations of the time. Their works remain inexhaustible storehouse of learning.

Children emulate their older siblings. What on earth induced political economy sprouts, economists, to act as if their predecessors were disoriented by their extrasensory awareness of their period and milieu? Nothing happens all at once; what seemed natural and exciting gradually trapped avaricious creatures. The political economy started to witness an outburst of skepticism. They broke rank from the standing army of naïve sympathizers who applauded the other canon and schools of reflective efforts to legislate against political and ethical regression despite paying a hefty price for their entr'acte and parochialism. Newcomers resisting compassion in their philosophic bricolage was, for moneyers, an act of bravery. A potent argument is that the pure treason prolonged the despair of the poor.

For the initial batch of economists, the quest for notoriety and respect did not consist of mere polished eloquence. They were more thrilled than obliged to deface political economists' gallant pleas and the humanistic impulse in order to enlist in hoodlums' crusades. The appeal of crossing to the wild analytical side was the desire to espouse the genuineness into what Thomas Carlyle and John Ruskin decried as a dismal science; or, as they bluntly state it, a gay science. The hype or illusion of scarcity was the currency abused by rogue political economy philosophers. It was believed that talented beings were rare; therefore, humans could not be equal. The truth was as simple as that. For the sake of humankind, exceptional and resilient men (the few) had to reign over the immature and pathetic mass permanently. Teams of sages bluntly affirmed that the souk should not synchronize the cadence of what commodities were worth, by quibbling. Such should be the responsibility of captains of industry. Cynical and degrading in public, the idea was stigmatized as false. However, in private, it was another story. Even though they did not get accolades or great reviews for spraying human waste on a canvas, they got uncanny adherents.

The total retreat of consciousness haggled down hominids' worth to stockpiles of muscles and mouths. Economics, or what was a commerce and trade subculture, flourished at the expense of the political economy by rejecting the relevance of the human soul. From that point on, in economics, the celebration of cerebral ejaculatio praecox became the fashion of the day. Manuscripts of early centuries embedded in oral traditions were hardly reliable.

Did other societies at any time scrutinize humans' caprices while trading off their needs and wants? Communities' deficits in transcriptions or surviving texts is held by others as evidence of their inability to reason. Streaming comes from the western hemisphere, manufacturing roar and demanding from newcomers the loyalty towards the nonfigurative to get a grip on the phenomena unleashed by the complexity of social actions filled with new art, economy, and cold-hearted bastards. Economists were more enthusiastic in their abominable principles than the political economists in the virtuous desires. When lumpen-intellectuals gawped in the past with their gray lenses, they asserted seeing Adam Smith's invisible soft hand, waving. It could well have been Barthélemy de Laffemas's middle finger.

> "Culture begets progress and without it cannot
> be required of people no moral conduct."
> —JOSÉ VASCONCELOS CALDERÓN

Evaluating if the world today is absurd or zanier than it has been, is no easy task. The sadness of mortal sins continually overwhelms ordinary souls. The simple truth is that if one is curious about the past, a perfect place to begin is by looking at history. Collectors rarely applied this critical test to their material. Traditions must be vandalized. Ancient world lunacies should get brighter with every disquisition as the factors contributing to civilizations rise and fall. Given the dialogic nature of human history, intertextuality is justified in passing judgment on the old days. The consistent disgust, anger, frustration, hatred, ambivalence, and apathy within humanity's relationships with the past have infused full-size deceits, circumventing facts and the contingency of context. This convention makes the past emerge comelier and perkier. The impulse of embellishing the old ways has been uninterruptedly in fashion. At some point in moving along history, we might realize that we are harboring stomach-turning ideologies by declining to defy our nostalgia. Yes, Casanova was a rapist!

We have come to witness a bold advance towards the philosophic interpretation of the life of humanity. There is dynamism and complementation between the past and the present, rather than vague coincidences. Refining the appraisal of the past permits other tones to be heard. If severe poverty, pandemic diseases, wars, ignorance, and spiritual exploitation are all primary parameters of measuring human progress, have we made any? What is there in the present day which doesn't exhibit perceptible religion influence in us? Bards and griots have not found a place among the great historians of the world. Hawks and vicious madmen are still role models. Are we willing to step back and make the wrong thing right?

Tuatha Dé Danann emerged from the gate to hell, taught Irish druidism, and exited from the same earth orifice. Screwballs inundated social and political economy in callousness and morphed into invisible monsters living today in our tap water. Their allegedly fresh theories like monotheism or division of labor were reconditioned, longstanding concepts, or the public prejudices and sentiments of their epoch. Theses rip-offs survived because of either the human body's proclivity for invisible, automatic processing, or because there wasn't a fashionably novel defense for obscure social construct.

These days, context and the collocation of emotion, time, and space have gotten a bad rap within academia. Political economist villains have constructed a magnificent bridge from the old prejudices to the new which is still the highway of discourses and stands erect long after every other idiotic tenet of the times have fallen into ruins. The law of the invisible shapes our fatuous optimism. Mercantilism is the whipping boy in the history of economics. Of the originators' intent or public prejudice of the epoch, the caput mortuum is what cunning economists display. It is not that the aroma and filthy essences, have vanished; but that we have become anosmatic.

We all know stories of somebody who did not want to lie, and was thrown in the furnace. The act of generosity comes after preventable horrors. Tears come down pale faces as the admiration of dead tyrants. The colonization bond between the oppressed and the oppressors pales in comparison to today's fiendish symbiosis between the abused and the abusers because of the melanin parity between the victims and the villains. The few who are gasping for freedom in shitty countries educe colonization proudly, with longing.

Up to the present millennium, Zhong Guo is a nation geographically disoriented, and can't figure how to get over the hump of being more than almost the supreme country on earth. Folks from shitty nations sing the Mowhee tune of seeking visas to the West to improve their fellow countrymen, when they merely want to live in a European society. The middle class liberates itself while it continues to gyrate to racist, misogynistic, and xenophobic cadence. The control by adult males of an excessively large shares of power is still a self-evident truth. What is the punishment of old white males misappropriating the work of their students, who were discriminated against? Nobel prizes.

As we conclude this chapter, a sad thought presses itself upon our minds: that our thirst for nonperishable evil acts is unquenchable. By its very nature, humanity's susceptibility to compassion acquired from miserable stretches is repetitively and harshly smashed. No one dares to betray the joints or reveal patches, because this will destroy the charm of innocence. We have not started to extol new heroes for new virtues. Spirituality stresses a rigid adherence to the shocking details that mock life. The public scoffs at scoundrels' ghoulish records and gushes over fickle deities who have long thrown in the towel and gone back to hell. The consolidation of gods surely reminisces of a time when the earth was not meandered by humans; the good ol' days.

3

Dumb and Dumber

"The almost insoluble task is to let neither the power of others,
nor our own powerlessness, stupefy us."
—THEODOR WIESENGRUND ADORNO

A LEAGUE OF ASSAULTS on life's constitutional dubiety has marginalized the prime driver of creativity. Revenants carry on ruining humanity's wisdom in its renewed embryonic stage. Tentacles of the persistent idiocy doctrine have the same devastating social bearing across the globe. The cynic dogmas always expand out of everyone's complacency. Attempts to sink villainy into oblivion should not be perceived as an act of heroism. No one deserve applauses for taking on the vicious psychosomatic monster of all. I am, myself, not innocent.

There was a time in my life when my tolerance was based on a naïve standard deviation of follies. I was just mildly discourteous to dummies who pat their own backs for democratizing a slum. I was not hypersensitive to imbeciles who swear that they do not see either race or gender. I should have used as a punching bag the face of idiots whose idea of improving living standards in war-ravaged regions is to allocate a pig to a family. Then again, it was hard, at the time, to fathom all psycho genes bottled in one zealot. One has to take time to eavesdrop on conversations throughout the socioeconomic pyramid to actually raise global devastation and self-awareness to an alien level.

Dare walk in any revered knowledge atelier, regardless if it is in the West, East, North or South, center, and you will be overwhelmed by the cyanic odor of dialectic bollocks. In these laboratories, upcoming financial czars, as well as international organizations' kingpins, proselytize the concept of marginal common sense. Their crappy model based on the white man burden and race hierarchy writes off from the equations paranoid despots and gluttonous buffoons. In doing so, the partial justice's derivative function approach dwarfs the psychological instability halting these poor nations' growth in commerce. Pathetic assumptions mold the interpretation of societal norms, commerce, and trade, and adds political neutrality to their moral depravity. There is no need to be worried about the stench of this puerile charter. The unparalleled mastering of the art of padding prejudice is squeaky clean.

There is an outrageous amount of energy squandered around the nerve-wrecking jingle "increase in wages automatically triggers the robotization of supermarkets and job cuts". Such claims have proven to be immaculately erroneous. The end of brown and dark people slavery, of child labor (in addition to shorter workdays), and employment benefits have demonstrated that human dignity and labor class exploitation successes are not mutually exclusive. I loathe minimum wage more than arrogant and judgmental billionaires. Where they and I are calling for the abolishment of minimum wage, I want to destroy the outdated notion that the ones at the bottom's lives have less value. I have yet to find solidarity towards my cause. The notion of minimum wage has made wealth distribution's schizophrenia highly functional. The betterment of labor attained without the slaving robots' illustration is an open hypocrisy at worst or mere inconsistency at best. It is imperative for robots to be enslaved and to replace human muscles and embarrassments in order to break the shackles off the minimum wage encumbrance.

What is there to say about inane celebrities' jaunts away from playing hero in the fantasy world to grapple with palpable social defiance? Two thumbs up to corporatism: these trendy crossovers hypnotize the public, swells the horrific "for the greater good" pseudo excuses, and spruces up absurdities. The standing ovation given to these jesters do nothing other than wreck the hopes of billions of souls in the dark world and sentimentalized ghettos. These unbearable spectacles do not awake common sense and firmness in dirt poor nations and banlieus. When all bets are off, humiliation and misery drive customarily sympathetic folks and defectors towards violent extremes: religion and guns! It should not come as a surprise to any well-balanced brain that inequality serves to further fuel the ire of those who've experienced injustice and provides a motive for shocking antiphons.

> "To write history is as important as to make history. If the writer
> does not remain true to the maker, then the unchanging truth
> takes on a quality that will confuse the humanity."
>
> —MUSTAFA KEMAL ATATÜRK

I am fed up with how, all over the globe, we come to eulogize Andrew Carnegie, John Pierpont Morgan Sr., John D. Rockefeller, and Cornelius Vanderbilt as great entrepreneurs. These despicable human beings have been crowned as The Men Who Put the Entire Globe on the Right Track. Their inflated goodwill has become the credo of cigar-capitalists' rationalization of widening the golden gates of pure evil, and for the decriminalization of greed. Voices condemning their evil tactics are the target of opprobrium. For this insult, I must credit my contemporary amnesia when it comes to the industrial revolution. There is no need to procure a shovel to unearth the trail of inhumaneness left behind from their wicked dealings and exploits. They consolidated supreme power and influence while aggressively stockpiling gems and collecting unnecessary prestige.

All over the globe, the attribute of a free market playing field bent on competitors' strangulation, their cadavers left behind for a corrupted head of state to bag and trash, is baleful. What Andrew Carnegie, J.P. Morgan, John D. Rockefeller, and Cornelius Vanderbilt called "bringing order in the chaotic system" was nothing other than halting the social revolution. Their pioneered business cartels are indeed cases of unnecessary, disgraceful evil. To get a sense of their commitment to renovated slavery and world domination, these malefactors financed a political heist and successfully got their pion, William McKinley, elected as the 25th U.S. President, who went on to roll back every regulation that stood in his benefactors' way, to pile up even more wealth. Today, this blueprint to amass mazuma and corner public policies has been rolled out all over the globe by these ever-covetous, affluent thugs.

The individuals consumed with guilt who stumbled into the White House to break ranks with the corrupt establishment were a source of opposition for the seething industrialists, and were instrumental to the twentieth-century social, commerce and trade, and political insurgency.

Antitrust beatings of the robber barons imposed new commerce traditions, or at least reversed the dehumanization of labor cycle. The situation also burst the door wide open for a new breed of less vicious business manipulators like Henry Ford. There is irrefutable evidence that the industrial revolution rat pack stagnated wealth distribution and social justice. Right after their monopoly was decapitated for the first time, white Americans were able to afford things that they made. The U.S. Industrial Revolution cannot be reconciled with academic integrity and the modern sanctioned, aesthetic, free market doctrine. And so, capitalism is not compatible with human and artistic growth and development.

In the present day, the backdrop of the American Civil War has been embellished with the heroic allegory of the northern free and enlightened states who pushed the tradition of humanism down the throats of southern slave and brutish states. It is one example of the powerful nations' puppeteers' common tradition of recoating history. Even though the truth has been obscured in the mists of partisanship going beyond the U.S. borders, it is never lost. For those who still have their heads, the U.S. Civil War was about two competing modes of exploitation, expected slavery in the south and accepted slavery in the north, over American territorial expansion to the Pacific coast as the spoils of the Mexican American war. The remnants of the U.S.'s pre-Civil War's inhuman and racialist customs are still violently experienced today.

To appreciate my devotion to anti-monopoly and to comprehend my devoutness to anti-privatization, it is deemed necessary to compartmentalize the two different sentiments. The thin and twisted rope connecting Arkansas to the Egyptians' remake of the Arab Spring that led to a multipart swap of modern-time pharaohs says a lot about our social interconnectivity. What we have today is the moral ground of antitrust laws that prevent one manic moneyer's hunger from blatantly gobbling up an entire sector of humans needs or wants. Instead, global paranoia has been used by international pillagers and their sponsors to break developing countries' safeguard nets and activate the foreignization of their national economies.

With one sailing across science and another crawling down the theological cliff, they will both end up disillusioned and insusceptible. It is a matter of time before one is sucked into political, highly subsidized scientific or religious idiocies. The human inability to sustain pain or avoid blame could lead us to look through rose-colored glasses, agonizing over historical events. In this shadowy painting of the world, how does a nonconformist mindset preserve an appropriate measure of sanity and integrity?

"No, Massa, it is best I had no learning,
for many learned men be great fools."

—NEGRO TOM

There is no shame in not knowing. This virtue is foreign to arrogance. An academic surgical dissection of beatified Los Pistorelos' classics do not lead a scaredy-cat to doubt of lumpen-intellectuals' holiness. Time can change contextual meaning, but not the intent. Plunging in the intent of extravagant claimants opens a can of blameless worms that indubitably humanized celebrated deities and undermined their legacy. For so long, the world was being fed numerous lies in order to underwrite social constructs. A wide range of ostentatious denigrations have become accepted as truth. Their longevity is born out of the modern peasants' dialectic complacency and the preposterousness of academic grandees.

Philosophy is an Olympian cerebral isometric, squeezing out authenticity from the basket of uncertainties. It is slated to be the ridiculous pursuit of understanding us, for self-awareness' sake. Folks in one part of the world intuitively picture unfamiliar spots as hotbeds of brutes. For inappropriate premises which are added to devious motives, Immanuel Kant has been crowned as the greatest philosopher of modern times. I sought his guidance to explain the origin of different human races, and particularly Negroes, as this was to become my cultural compass.

"The growth of the spongy parts of the body had to increase in a hot and humid climate. This growth produced a thick, turned-up nose and thick, fatty lips. The skin had to be oily not only to lessen the too heavy perspiration, but also to ward off the harmful absorption of foul, humid air. The profusion of iron particles which are otherwise found in the blood of every human being and, in this case, is precipitated in the net-shaped substance through the evaporation of the phosphoric acid (which explains why all Negroes stink), is the cause of the blackness that shines through the epidermis. [. . .] Besides all this, humid warmth promotes the strong growth of animals. In short, all of these factors account for the origin of the Negro, who is well-suited to this climate: namely being strong, fleshy, and agile. However, because his motherland so amply supplies him, he is also lazy, indolent, and dawdling." [1]

1. Bernasconi, Robert, and Tommy Lee Lott, eds, *The idea of race*, 17.

Right now, I need to pause. All marsupials delegated to the species lower on the totem pole, please allow me to get on Kant's stupidity level by sensationalizing Cheikh Anta Diop's counterpunch Two Cradle Theory. My depiction of Kracker's origin is:

> "The dwindling of the spongy parts of the body had to be caused by cold and dry climate. This degeneration produced a thin, protruding, beak pointed nose and thin lips. The skin had to be dry and translucent, as a protective measure due to poor hygienic practices, and, in this case, in case they get wet the thick waste coating the epidermis is diluted (which explains why all Krakers smell like wet dogs). Besides all this, dry cold promotes homosexuality. In short, all of these factors account for the origin of the Kracker, who is well-suited to this climate; namely, gangly, aggressive, with a disgust for existence, pessimism, the enslavement of women, and moral depravations. However, because his arid and cold environment does not yield long-term subsistence, he is also sadistic, parochialistic, and hysterical. "

If you applaud my basest retort, then you are a Neanderthal. Claims can be constructed to account for East Asian slanted eyes or to generalize about unpleasant Arab breath. In the same spirit of the Hippocratic Oath, not harm, the scientific inquiry should refrain itself from providing asinine evidence to offensive stereotypes. Albert Einstein claimed that racism is a disease of white people. He ignored or had no clue about other races' bigotries—Japan's notion of ethnic purity, or the idea that Russian blacks are not necessary black. Poor indigenous people in Bolivia cultivate pity and disdain for blacks. Black Africans frown upon any female who consorts with white men. Another overrated and over-cited phantom, David Hume (whom I assumed wasn't aware of the Sankore University, which was established in the early 1300s in Timbuktu), wrote:

> "I am apt to suspect the Negroes and in general all other species of men (for there are four or five different kinds) to be naturally inferior to the whites. There never was a civilized nation of any other complexion than white, nor even any individual eminent either in action or speculation. No ingenious manufactures amongst them, no arts, no sciences. On the other hand, the rudest and barbarous of the whites, such as the ancient GERMANS, the present TARTARS, have still something eminent about them in their valor, the form of government, or some other particular."[2]

2. Hume, *Of National Characters*, 225.

There is consistency in beatified Caucasian analytical heroes in the racism marathon. Every race deserves a medal of completion for their contribution to this absurd saga. Ibn Khaldun is an African who firmly believed that geometry enlightens the intellect and sets one's mind right. He is often viewed as one of the godfathers of modern economics, especially monetary economics (yuck). The man is credited with observing and articulating the benefit of the division of labor in his book, Kitab al-Ibar, long before Adam Smith wrapped it around the concepts pocketed from the French physiocrats. In addition, Khaldun brilliantly introduced the labor theory of value centuries ahead of David Ricardo. He also blurted:

> "Beyond to the south, there is no civilization in the proper sense. There are only humans who are closer to dumb animals than to rational beings. They live in thickets and caves and eat herbs and unprepared grain. They frequently eat each other. They cannot be considered human beings."[3]

Every century seems to start and end with Western bigoted synthesis reigning supreme over the universe. In the middle of the journey, the entirety of humanity pours excessive veneration upon disgraceful human beings appointed as the great thinkers of their time. The most despicable case has to be Gandhi. I am deeply disturbed every time Mahatma Gandhi is politely called the "Great Soul" by anyone who is not bravely wearing a swastika sign. The unrepentant pedophile offered jurisprudence to the Indians in South Africa under the apartheid system. He believed in the purity of races. For Bapu, Indians were undoubtedly inferior to Caucasians, but he lamented that:

> "We could understand not being classed with whites, but to be placed on the same level as the Natives seemed too much to put up with. Kaffirs are as a rule uncivilized—the convicts even more so. They are troublesome, filthy and live like animals."[4]

There is a sickening inconsistency in the John Locke, the 'Father of Liberalism', and the Enlighted François-Marie Arouet (Voltaire) assertion that all men are equal while benighted perspective of reason by investing heavily their cash in the slave trade. But the French aristocrat Joseph Arthur is an alarming example of the far-reaching costs of prolonging prejudicial hypotheses. With no clue on how to conduct scientific research, he became

3. Khaldun, *The Muqaddimah*, 319–20.

4. Lelyveld, *Great Soul*, 74.

marvelously famous for developing the theory of the Aryan master race. He bundled up people by their skin colors and affirmed that intelligence quotient is determined by genetic inheritance. And the Third Reich made his irrational mantra a centerpiece of their orchestrated carnage. Today, lowlife skinheads and vacuous scientific racists and misogynists chant out the rash suspicion to provide grounds for a commitment to absurdity that's enshrined within academia.

A good breakthrough cannot be expected by merely appealing to people's existing traditions. In the West, East, North, and South, scientific prejudice runs deep in academia's veins. Bias is a pettifogging moral imbalance as value significances fluctuate. On the other hand, prejudicial behavior inflicts severe damage upon the entire society that seeks to deprive another individual's social equity. As we stay on the same dance floor, we can predict, with the highest degree of certainty, the worsening of social injustice and recurring commerce and trade tragedies on a global scale.

> "Only to the rude ear of one who is quite indifferent does the
> song of a bird seem always the same."
>
> —ROSA LUXEMBURG

The prolonged effect of this synthetic omnipotence pales in comparison to the shift in the ravaging clandestine war over the control of homo genus' minds. The whipping gain made by science over religion was credited for the moderation of bigotry, racism, sexism, slavery, and other flamboyant absurdities. Other results are perplexing. Contemporary scientific triumphs have led to the intellectualization of every conversation. In this craze, Western cognoscenti is believed to be infallible, and its by-blows are viewed as deities in the enclaves of academic ghettos around the globe. You might be puzzled by Kant, Hume, Diop, Gandhi, and Khaldun's racist verbal diarrhea. How could such highly esteemed canvassers of human comportments and luminescence be capable of such terrible ignorance?

When people attempt to preserve traditional crafts, we ought to applaud their efforts. The past enriches contemporary culture. In some instances, we ought to take extreme measures to correct historical glitches. People like Kant and Hume, just to name the few, and the iconic prejudices embedded in their works have had an untold amount of devastating damage for centuries. Rendering their whole kit and caboodle null more than sets an example or a warning to other bellicose scientific racists. It ends the applause for their mischief and possibly cures humanity of cogent argument's dysentery. Who is Eugen Karl Dühring?

Every injustice ruse relies heavily on psychology in order to manipulate the collective wisdom into believing in the illusion of rightness. Unless you have been in the trenches, staring at economic academia without intimidation, you are undoubtedly wondering about the specific charges which I pose against capitalism. These are different from the current caseload and exhibits you have become desensitized to. It is no easy task to turn the switch on underpinning problems which I am jabbing into your brain. To burst your constellation-like view or bubble, I should fall back to history and lure you into a dreadful act of treason and stupidity galore: Dred Scott vs. Sandford (1857).

Less than a century after Olaudah Equiano published his memoir, Dred Scott, a Negro, attempted to sue for his freedom in the basis of his extended stay with his owner in states and territories where slavery was illegal. In framing his case in such an awful way, he ratified the idea that being human is not a thing all human beings are all entitled to by virtue of simply being human: dumb! In this landmark decision, the U.S. Supreme Court denied Scott's request and stipulated that neither he nor any other person of African ancestry could claim citizenship in the United States because they were properties, like a chair or a pig: dumber!

In Scott's mind (and the U.S. Supreme Court at that time), unless a group of living human beings fulfills ambiguous prerogatives of being human, they are objects. I have no sympathy for Scott, for he had no intention of taking down slavery. If he was admitted to being a free man, I wager that he would have exercised the privilege of being human and purchased his own slaves. I would not expect anything else from a judicial system that is still trying to find its way back to bigoted days. Throughout the ninetieth and twentieth centuries, lumpen-intellectuals have been galloping all over the globe, delivering an intense harangue to vindicate social, commerce and trade, and political class ranks. They perpetuate social injustices of any form as a normal consequence of nature. For them, we are nothing more than a disposable means of production, and only a small number of us (the rich) are special creatures; human beings. In these days and times, this mephitic evangel has gained more scholastic grounds. The ninety-nine percenters still foolishly upholding this sordid and mortifying social construct are dumb and dumber!!!

4

The Usual Suspects

"There must always be a remedy for wrong and injustice
if we only know how to find it."

—IDA B. WELLS

ON THE SURFACE, THE present-day phase of humankind has nothing in common with the heartlessness and insanity of the past. For good reason, one could conclude that it should not take long mental preparation to dazzle the ancient Romans. Slaves were forced to fight to the death against another slave or a wild animal for the entertainment of the spectators. Nothing set us apart from these primitive hooligans in the way we gobble up scholarly guano. Despite the fact that the number of deities is dwindling closer to one (money), our pretext for propitiatory child sacrifices is not far different from Moloch worshipers. Our unwavering worship of psychopath politicians, religious elitists, and boorish moneyers (or, just call them deputized pricks) shows that we are still enthusiastically primitive.

On the macabre global journey of integrity neutering, bright sparks are filling the universe. Social resentments have been simmering. We are phenomenally winning the fight against death. Some individuals take it upon themselves to persistently harass society's normalcy by italicizing irrationalities and brutalities. Dissenters ridicule social, commerce and trade, and political conventions. In many ways, the history of the world is like human poop. It is simple to think of feces as the vestiges of what you gobbled up. In reality, there is more to the configuration of your dung: excluding water, more than fifty percent is bacteria that have been carousing in your intestines. During the poop discharge, many of the bacteria in poop die shortly afterward. In hominid evolution, moral failings do not face the same fate. The incomplete progression is at the root of the global consciousness stagnation.

Once voices for social justice gain popularity, cliques of megalomaniacs join the laypeople to hijack the celebration with an air of haughtiness. In defiance, dialecticians mitigate the impact of the mutiny on mainstream analysis and sentience. Moneyers reproach prescient warnings as unfounded and demagogic. These are individuals and groups who greatly benefit from social and political arrangements pervading the stench of misery. The legion of pantaloons swirls enchanting words and befuddles slothful souls unapprised of the new paradigm shift. So as not to be outdone, one-eyed Goliaths give the impression of being relevant and more concerned with the correct literary elements than with what is being said. Meanwhile, archeologists spend considerable time and energy searching for the oldest human feces.

My contemporary's portrayal of the world we live in has roiled the bastion of hypocrisy. Consider that less than a century after World War II, we brazenly flirt with the absurd depiction of Adolf Hitler as a visionary and messiah. Some romantics go even further, highlighting the sanctions imposed after World War I to exonerate Germany's hell on earth and the Schutzstaffel's crime against humanity. To top these insolences, Germans of that era are, in the same fable, mocked as adolescents who innocently embraced and jubilated two cornerstones of any national sense of exceptionalism, die Herrenrasse, and Lebensraum. The implicit gullibility is inconsistent with the sustained German sentiment of racial perfectionism.

In a probe of the interpretations of social dilemmas and the recommended treatments, one astutely muses about the scientific manure mix of alcohol and herbs that lumpen-intellectuals indulged in before blurting out cerebral diarrhea. The stars are the ones the least comprehended, and have the best arsenal of old sermons. Mysticism and foolishness have been overused to fill the sinkholes of apathy. Theological maxims are the most seductive instruments used to prolong public lassitude and are enthused behemoths' usual modus operandi in the subjugation of the masses. The extended and expanded esoteric theoretical disputes and the hebetude of universal minds keep on smashing social aspirations.

In a sincere attempt to close this segment on a good note, we should pat ourselves on the back for the continued crafting of a sense of sureness. It fortifies the apathetic attitude of the public. The avalanche of assault on common sense disintegrates public appreciation and gives encouragement to insurgents. The tactic successfully contains our urge to petition for social and political changes. The inquiry into pure idiocy, like eugenics in the past, tells us one thing: the price of snubbing social mores mutinies far exceeds the cost to our collective conscience.

I do not trust the slow mental process to untangle my morbid humor. In some respects, the effort to eradicate human callousness is silly. We live and die by obfuscated social, commerce and trade, and political pacts. It will be a disservice to you if I delegate to apatheists the task of disemboweling accepted norms. Be aware, as I am approaching becoming downright offensive.

> "I did not join the resistance movement to kill people,
> to kill the nation. Look at me now. Am I a savage person?
> My conscience is clear."
>
> —SALOTH SAR

Capitalism has been patented as the best mechanism of offering every single partaker equal rights and equal opportunities. Involuntary human servitude, slavery, was still the regular part of life for unaccredited humans when this social, commerce and trade, and political arrangement erupted onto the scene. We have since given a new touch and signature mark to overextended oppression. One was to be born into slavery and die in slavery. In our time, one is to come into life in and perish in an innovative and romanticized form of slavery. On capitalism's watch, doctrinal variances and the social agony perpetual are often lost in the sea of moneyers and their devoted abettors' schemes.

The list of Western elitists' deprecatory arguments of why billions of people are soaked in terrible poverty is too long. There was a time when a fair trade was a fair exchange. Westerners brought smallpox to the new world. In exchange, they got syphilis. For hipsters, the antidote to commerce and trade injustice is fair trade. None of these effete brains seem to notice critical aspects of countries on the bottom of the shit list; one which involves Western powerhouses constantly choreographing the purge of developing nations' sense of social orientation and aspirations. To think for a minute that fair trade promotes safe, healthy working conditions, protects the environment, enables transparency, and empowers communities to build strong, thriving businesses is preposterous; not to mention revolting. The fair-trade crusade's single amusing exploit is the bimbos' pageantries in forgotten and forsaken parts of the world. Western governments' pervasive meddling cements the global commerce and trade status quo in weak nations' affairs. Fair trade is just another classic nauseating gimmick to secure capitalism's imperium, or, simply put, a social, commerce and trade, and political shime-waza technique.

Fair trade skullduggery pales in comparison to another tall tale: the causality between cost-cutting and prices. Production cost must be chopped to the bones in order for individuals to meet the expense of their wants to the detriment of another's. There is something wrong with the mark in the universal acceptance of this hunchback of commerce and trade. This buyer-sanctioned delusion and the tongue-tied nations' pledge to poverty conveniently flushes out any remorse while mesmerizing the pile of waste we produce. Every scheme of cost cutting's result is surplus increase and quality decrease. Expense reduction schemes make the rich richer and cheat on the poor. It is long overdue to recognize that the cost-cutting obsession is spoiling the ecosystem and human taste.

Now and then, the death toll of capitalism's disasters keeps us up at night. Melodramatic and sporadic suicides in Chinese industrial units blot out the epidemic Karōshi in Japan. People are literally working themselves to death. What do the unspeakable tragedies of the twenty-first century Tazreen Fashions Factory in Bangladesh and the twenty century Triangle Shirtwaist Factory in the United States have in common? The doors to the stairwells and exits were sealed to prevent workers from taking unauthorized breaks and pilfering. Cost cutting and fair-trade moral hazard arguments have a pungent and savory flesh. Moral issues imbroglio is weighed down by crackerjack prevaricators. Considering other egregious human costs, neither crooks' conspiracies nor melodramatic factories' scenes are the points of concurrency of capitalism's travesties. The capitalism poison is brewed out of troupers' primitive greed, regimes' appetite for grandeur, and vultures' chic voracity.

> "Death laid its eggs in the wound."
> —FEDERICO DEL SAGRADO CORAZÓN
> DE JESÚS GARCÍA LORCA

Prosperity's artifices are bestrewn with banderoles crediting the free market for everything. These global affluence illusions have come to legitimize planned obsolescence. As soon the refurbished concepts fade and the world faces recurring commerce and trade slumps, moneyers bring the circus into town. Everyone gets a dozen free passes to watch clumsy Blemmyae, spending devotees, pinned against maniacal Sciopods and austerity cliques. These eerie wrestling spectacles successfully dissolve every attempt at a sincere dialog on surplus sharing into pretentious rhetoric. Occasionally, the austerity code of Hammurabi and spending mooring tussles spin out of control into a series of gruesome rendezvous with death. Long gone is the time when masterminds of austerity measures and protagonists of spending were physically squashed away. More than the sense that we are notoriously blasé about tragedies when gazing upon them from afar, our predilection to the round-the-clock celebration of the concocted "années folles" holds muted diabolical clashes.

Austerity jingles and spending monkeyshines are veils for protecting the moneyers' interests. Various academic orders of knighthood tweak piles of rotting hallucinatory shreds of evidence to flaunt their amorality and arouse moneyers. All these various and wildly divergent desperadoes start their ratiocination on the same decent premise: people have different gifts. From the liberal argument, they juice out a hideous moralizing discourse which implies that moneyers are go-getters utilizing their innate talents. The claim of only a few chosen ones worthy of far more than any imaginary compensation adds zest to mass manipulation. A tiny number of supermen, namely moneyers, have a mix of divine frugality and chromosomal predisposition to make the necessary sacrifice to accumulate stupefying wealth. Then there is the rest: ordinary mortals who do not have the aforementioned characteristics. These "other" humans have an inherent moral imperfection to indulge in debaucheries and go on shopping sprees that shackle them to perpetual agony. They are righteously entitled to a minuscule portion of the surplus generated from any enterprise. The nonsensicality of this tale is a blatant disregard of income accruals: dwarfism, in contrast to their wealth enlargement haste. It is the classic case of hanging the victim. The bad news is that this corny satire, which at once glorifies and trivializes social prejudice, is a worldwide hit, and too often used to smear nations and an entire hemisphere.

A glance at the jaw-dropping debts of developed nations or the perplexing balance sheet of the rich debunks the abstinence myth. In fact, the entire rigged commerce and trade mechanism is fashioned to reward big spenders and to torment small hoarders. There are as much a priori truths as a posteriori argument evidencing that poor folks and shitty nations are mere bystanders to capitalism's global financial massacres. For a nation that aspires to break poverty cycle, this is a simple formula. You must spend or crook your way into the elite club of nations granted immunity against poverty. Once your financial recklessness exceeds a ridiculous level, you will get knighted as too white or too obese to go on a financial diet. Don't forget to order in the elite club catalog the diamond-encrusted gold ring with encryption: "He who will not economize will not have to agonize."

"The poor people are those who suffer, are sentenced to jail,
and die without shedding tears."

—NAJI SALIM HUSSAIN AL-ALI

I have this deep-seated aversion to two melodramatic phrases, "the gods have spoken" and "God, in his infinite wisdom," which far exceed my distaste of the words "slavery" and "obedience." Throughout human recorded existence, when deities are viewed as more than cavalcade mascots, terrible things happen. There is no worse irrational process or sequence of logical fallacies that is harder to break away from or to revoke, once it begins with or chains its legitimacy to "God." Critical thinking and debate do not involve appeals to the supernatural.

As capitalism powerhouses hit the skids and Western commerce and trade stunts fall flat, Islamic economists cheered and shouted out: "I told you so." There is a paucity of evidence that calls into question the merits of the bitter Middle Eastern lumpen-intellectual parade. Members of any ulema are prohibited from juxtaposing Islamic economics with conventional economics. The fear of being accused of blasphemy and mocking Islamic faith dissuade informed knockers from exposing the arrangement of cognitive dissonance. To your delight, I am a wayward social faultfinder. In accordance to my sharia laws, juiced from an astute Persian observer sermon: "it is not worth the life of poverty for the sake of faith or ideology", I am now granting you and myself full immunity against any dialectic fatwa. An explanation of how anything works must be defensible without invoking a supernatural being. I have said it before, and I will repeat it: "Socialism, fascism, and communism have failed, but now capitalism is strangling us." I have held Islamic economics' delusional parasitosis at bay in order for my anxiety and augury to reach an unbiased absolute and make this journey more intoxicating.

Islamic economics is described as a vibrant set of laws for settling disputes. A survey of exciting terms to enunciate on the list of Sukuk like Musharakah, Mudarabah, Shirkat-ul-milk, and Skirkat-ul-aqd unveils the system's obsession with accommodating all aspects of moneyers' stings. In fact, every Sukuk has a similar tool in capitalism. Besides, the abuse and fierceness of financial instruments such as future options trading and its derivative in Islamic commercial jurisprudence are the same as in capitalism. The prohibition of riba, equating it to zulm, is the most ludicrous concept of all its charades. A revolting sentiment toward Islamic economics builds up once one realizes that the standard Islamic financing mechanisms Murabahah and Ijaarah (which are merely rent-to-own arrangements) allow banks to charge up to hundred percent fixed interest.

In theory, Islamic commercial jurisprudence precludes discrimination based on gender, religion, region, and ethnicity. There is nothing off about the idea that people have different levels of talent. These underpinnings are suitable for primary use in sculpting priceless and logical artifacts in a capitalistic culture. The exhibition of decorum takes a back seat when "bestowed by God" is added to the tail of social constructs. The rationalization of injustice is without proof to back diety directives. Islamic economics is a strong case of the demoralizing consequences of marring political economy mantra with spirituality. The socio-threatening hyperemia in this model is anticipatable, in particular, in the way surplus is dispersed amongst active participants of an enterprise.

In the Islamic commercial parable, on one side, the moneyers' gangs of Rabbul-mal, Mudarib, and Karimis, because of their superhuman attributes, get their chunk of the surplus in percentage. On the other side, the Kasik and Ajir live off meager residuals of the surplus. Islamic psychitzophrenic economics postulates that the entire planet depends on labor for survival. At the same time, it ties labor compensation to the provision of service and moneyer caprices. The different analysis tosses Ecir (the private worker) and Ecir-i müşterek (the ordinary worker) into the laboring class. By disjointing the laboring class compensations from great harvests, a luxury granted to moneyers, the system subjugates Ecir and Ecir-i Müşterek to despair. If you are scratching your head trying to figure why this derangement does not sound familiar to you, well, this is the same as in capitalism.

Hence, in a nutshell, Islamic economics parallels capitalism. Both ensure surplus distribution discrimination and canonize moneyers. Capitalism stretches the rights and privileges established by the Magna Carta

Libertatum to barons, creatures considered humans in the thirteenth-century, and left-out serfs. Commercial and trade circulation patterns using the teachings of Islam are embedded in similar archaic religious diktats from which human bondage customs were built on. These right refinement results were more effective at suppressing social progress. Furthermore, the undeniable sad truth punches through once the pious mascara is peeled off. Capitalism is nothing more than an Islamic economics copycat; an amoral dogma backed by theological aberrations that vindicate vassalage. More importantly, capitalism's apostles and Islamic economics disciples unrepentantly accept as true the mandatory gap between the poor and the rich to generate a harmonious social, commerce and trade, and political arrangement in a society. Basouma lé kaskia; Inch 'Allah!

"I alone knew what I had suffered.
I alone knew what it felt like to be alive but dead."
—PHOOLAN DEVI

Early political economy pontiffs' tracts are indubitably persistent dialectic exertions to study carefully and thoroughly the pandemonium of production and trade. Has humanity made any progress? There is indeed a finger on the pulse of what was going on around their world. What is often forgotten is that they were more than pollsters of commerce conversion. They alerted society on social anomalies and swayed political verdicts. They bravely articulated unviable social, commerce and trade, and political frameworks that haunt us today. Their prestige also facilitated the rise of political economy within philosophy and paved the way for further developments.

The cause of the social, commerce and trade, and political periodic cyclones and the spray of overextended misery are easily expunged if we could deadbolt absurd lips and cockamamie theories. Excommunicating imbeciles will result in nothing if we cannot dichotomize disparity and injustice. It is where the political economy has lost its virility. Since nature does not tolerate a vacuum, absurdities have filled in the proper space. So goes the finger pointing in one direction: no matter what triggered a financial blizzard, lumpen-intellectuals concoct a racketeering charge indicating the poor. For moneyers, it is the poor who are always the cause of all that comes from capitalism's troubles, as well; and from the next, and so on. For laborers, it is the rich who are always the cause of every chaos, as well; and from the next, and so on.

Diagnostic: Sleeping Is Taunting Death

Social construct anomalies are created by parasites. I do not care about any form of disparity for the simple reason that they are structural gaps inherent to nature. I cannot, per contra, hold back from shaming commerce and trade evils or single out any socio-politico deliria cases. I cannot stress this enough: we have the potential to be good or bad. Some milieus and settings are breeding grounds for the evil in all of us. The repugnant leading inequality is learned intolerance. To puke the argument with a better aroma, I shall say that injustice of any form is not a moral failing, but rather a prodrome of abysmal social constructs such as patriarchy, theism, and every flamboyant commerce and trade awful tenet. Hence, poverty and every "ism" silliness are alarming signs of social pathogens. Taken in this context, by proscribing human body parts auctions, defacing Jesus Halverde shrines, shaming the Restavek institution, blowing up psycho mujahedeen, oppressing Uyghurs on their ancestral land, or restyling sakoku, we have been whipping the wrong horse on and on and on.

Veritas

Life Is the Leading Cause of Death

5

Econometricks

"The layer that is above the sky and below the earth, which is described as being situated between the earth and the sky and which is indicated as the symbol of the past, present, and future, where is that situated?"

—GARGI VACHAKNAVI

OBSESSION AND DELUSION INTERSECT where the supernatural flourishes. Humans are perturbed by matters of the spirit in relationship to the body. Convicts were the first to be dismembered to assess the intricacy of human anatomy. A significant amount of concern to avoid awakening a feature shared by all beings may sound bizarre outside the ruminations of the metaphysical, yet great care is taken to acknowledge the existential. In the old days, in order to not interfere with afterlife symbioses, the corpse was expected to be draped with only the body part exposed for excision. This ancient paranoia which persists today gave birth to a medical model that subscribes to the notion of the mystic's role in life. The same goes for the inexhaustible index of spiritual opinions to substantiate cruelty toward the low-rung working class. More than in the much-admired European social pyramid, the Motu Proprio Magnum Principium was being used by disciples of naturalistic inquiry to nuke those who engaged in social activism.

So much would have been evident to obscurantists of capitalism's nascent stage, where intellectualizing inhumanity received high praises and favors. As calamities worsen, the consequences are not what is expected:

pundits' fanaticism swells the general public's indisposition to mental effort. With a large pool of cocksuckers and audacious lumpen-intellectuals, political economy has been relegated to a passive observer's role in economics. A seemingly coherent hodgepodge of nonsense and decadent analytical twiddles were shackled to political economy synthesis to incubate an ambiguous science. This spineless accord has germinated commerce and trade convolutions.

Economics appropriated the right and privilege of the social, commerce and trade, and political trinity's noble alliance. The concerted effort of subduing emotion out of humanity can be traced back to one of the earliest secret societies. Titivated legacies praising the penchants and constraints of tricksters straddled the line between innocence and malice. Ideological moorings constrict comprehensive liberation schemas. Sophists knew all too well to ground their prejudices into conventional wisdom, where discretion must be tussled out of ordinary folks' evidence processing steps. As soon as you eat their canard, you turn blind; there is no going back to see through the malarkey. Vain assumptions used as a premise for mathematical equations have ransacked morality and sympathy.

Antonio Gramsci mistook the mid-twentieth century class of cerebral desperadoes for organic intellectuals. There is nothing organic about lumpen-intellectuals. We are to thank technological forays for shedding light on past and persistent rotten events. The 1960s' schmaltzy era failed to tone down the absurd hypothesis explosion. The masters staked out unequivocal positions; power and influence were kept on their side of the chess board. The northern hemisphere did not move to eradicate champions of other parts of the world. The shocking muggings of reason had a dreadful human life price tag. Billions of children, women, and men were deprived of any dignity. International organizations' unrealistic directives on global affairs invited trouble from régimes naturally inclined to profligacy. Free-market and spiritual evangelists unperturbedly ganged up to succor Western moneyers' reign over the rest. Lost lives were painted out as the collateral damage of Beelzebub's will.

It is a moral duty to warily strip-search the underpinnings of a principle before pledging allegiance to it. Not just pickpockets and swindlers lend value to diversions. The advantage of mathematics in every analysis is rolled around the postulation as the right tool for scholars to express themselves in a precise and straightforward way. Nonconformists who endeavored to extol the virtues of Marxism did not halt the zentai philosophy invasion of social research or the gerrymandering of hypotheses and trends. A new breed of ostentatious economics' jugglers ornate their cupolas with equations and charts.

In every scientific field, numbers are eccentrically perceived as the correct way to stitch and maintain social order. Experts are explicitly emboldened to mimic accuracy by sculpting data as the sole proper means for persuasion. Econometrics' firm grip on good sense and sound judgment is not the pejorative evidence that the truth has ceased to be necessary for belief. The application of statistical methods to commerce and trade data has subjugated social discourses into a language that few speak and tweak. Blasting away human sentiments to erect a potent theory has engendered an enduring sense of confusion. In essence, the active campaign of repressing feelings in meticulous exploration is making academics dumbly numb.

> "The supporter of ornament believes that the urge for simplicity
> is equivalent to self-denial."
> —ADOLF FRANZ KARL VIKTOR MARIA LOOS

Every civilization has a hysterical faith in the existence of beings with the power to halt common decency's dilapidation and the human race self-destruction. The second half of the twentieth century kickstarted with a social groan and clank from infuriated and invigorated revolutionaries and chauvinists around the world. Amid violent clashes, some theoreticians sought to stimulate another kind of conversation. For these enthused genii, there was a pressing need to figure out, once and for all, if there are intelligent creatures lost in space or lonely in a galaxy far, far away. Two elements sketched out of these overly-trained minds on a napkin are at the same time charming and perplexing. 'N' is the number of groups out there that would better schmooze than enslave us. 'L' assumes that these creatures with an antenna on their head and one eye would be eager to let us know that they are in the neighborhood. The Fermi paradox's simplicity should have sent to the grave the Drake equation; yet, it has endured. Abstract spasms are embedded in these kinds of inane pursuit. Besides, climacophobia is the result of daring to disprove that we cohabit earth with other humanlike colonies, but in different dimensions.

The 1960s are irrefutably the costliest years regarding general principle blunders. It is archaeologically the most perilous step in the wrong direction in the partisan and commercial arena. The neoclassical economists magnificently imbued the discourse with mathematical tricks that slew common sense in social, commerce and trade, and political hypothesis. Mastering the science of perfumery is an essential part of operating in the modern world. Mathematics' fallacy competence lies in its ease of camouflaging analytical trash in plain sight. If only every skinhead, dogmatist, and aged being were busy looking up to the sky, looking for any sign of extraterrestrial life creatures that could well downgrade humans to kings and queens of the jungle, the world would have been a better place; but only the very few of them at the extreme edges do so. The ubiquitous influence of mathematics on the modern favorite commerce and trade autopsy method of economics, a field colonizing social and politic discourses, has had dire implications.

Pictures and words can complement each other. Pictures have solely driven economics. When anyone reaches the summit of the illusion, one ceases to observe rather than vindicate. On the last stretch of higher learning, students are trained to formulate a question for the sake of it, which defies the notion of solving an issue. These acolytes' career aim is to concoct a model of discolored tendency. When presented with two disasters, highly trained minds who think faster than someone else can speak will project the story in ratios. The excuse is that it is the only way to provide the validity and reliability necessary for social planning and commerce and trade resolutions. Ordinary mortals will ask how a string of occurrences unfolded. Chopping up an observation in numbers is said to make sense when there is a proper conviction that an event could occur again. Rising social class tensions means fewer members of the elite are at ease with the political and economic status quo. Apathy intensified with research ventures out farther into the abstract to make a case for moneyers.

One set of principal architects of the political economy's primary concern of society is take care of the poor while the most dynamic group sought to protect the minority of the prosperous against the majority. Will-o'-the-wispy economics' personages gained notability and made a ruse out of the yardstick for sculpting models. The daftest postulation has been the one that begets the highest esteem. Often, what is deemed qualitative information does not aid in developing a complete understanding. The hierarchical model is solely driven by pictograph descriptions of statistical modeling without the diverse narratives of realities for the sake of the ever-elusive generalization stamp of approval. It should be a warning to all of us to look at the concept of general systems theory with a grain of salt and, in turn, consider the human patterns connected to its specifics of cultures, norms, and values.

There is seldom no resistance to changing the current path we cling to, like the mythical lemming over the cliff analogy as it pertains to crowds. Wise-looking beings turn up to support the claim that capitalism is the only right way in many respects, when moneyers are losing control over society. Individuals who see all the arguments for the free market become blind to the arguments against it. To break the poor solidarity and to can-onize moneyers, a new breed of slave traders has kept up with their mission of exorcising the emotions out of people's heads. These deductions leave out the fact that sympathy toward the less fortunate is a human trait. The full story needs to be told.

Timorous practitioners can open-endedly sputter and indulge in the theatrical. Politics is the area where the misuse of statistics is expected. The doleful public plea to bedazzle and insatiable academic demand for con-tributions to a field have amplified the stream of bullshit. Institutions re-sponsible for endocrine in the youth—or, simply put, factories that produce human algorithms—have modernized the process of the aptitude matura-tion steps of developing hypotheses. Set on the field partialities or a patron agenda, a pollster nitpicks data to dissect the problem and concoct the answer. This technique guarantees the stress-free delivery of a gorgeously bogus recommendation. In essence, it is all about flashing a view, teasing it with an exact opposite, and the collage of other performers' sound bites. It is terrifying that economics dons have gained more power and influence, but have followed somewhat the same paths during the past few decades. The difference between other fields and economics is that their paddocks can sustain goof-ups, while their recent antics perpetuate injustice and claims lives.

> "Everything can be explained to the people, on the single condi-
> tion that you really want them to understand."

—FRANTZ OMAR FANON

A shady lifestyle certainly pulls away from a lasting peace of mind. The twentieth century was dominated increasingly by mathematical analysis and the abuse of deductive logic. The folly took another step when math-ematics was added to economics drawings, which should be regarded as a beautiful, poisonous rose. Human personality was stiffed with an eidolon of solid probabilities. The opportunity resulted in intensified possibilities of anxiety. Somehow, a correlation got wedded to causality, sealing two unrelated observations' fates. A single occurrence was customarily stretched to arouse disciples.

The tale of the correlation between baldness and heart attack is particularly fascinating. The amount of cerebral power that has been wasted to argue one way or another makes one wonder if this is anti-Christian pagan revivalism or a shred of evidence on Homo sapiens' inability to find a way out of pervasive social, commerce and trade, and political injustice shackles. The political hostility between the Soviet bloc countries and the US-led Western powers was an incinerator of equality's ideals. We ought to crown the 1960s unequivocally as the particular decade in which the vagaries birthed out of it have prolonged and intellectualized social, commerce and trade, and political idiocy.

First and foremost, this period juxtaposed two passionate paradoxes. Western conspicuous voices successfully winched up awareness on the exceptional cruelty and prejudice that gangrened human interactions. Their melancholic ballads reached a wider Western audience, and their sympathy toward what was painted as shitty people and places grew some cojones. On the other corner of the same stage, dastardly bigotries were being candy-coated with irrational panic and jingoism. The only way to tell the truth is to tell the truth; albeit, it can be stressful. On the other hand, the daunting array of readily accessible information has worsened the complexity of dissecting events as they happen, and has blurred past events. The exasperation of cracking a signal safely out of noise should be the golden motive to take on a seemingly impossible effort to solve issues. Instead, we institutionalized scholarly indolence, made belief the truth-bearer, and placated knowledge that genuinely vindicates propositions.

It is easy to say that agony, devastation, cruelty, and farewell arouse spirits of a past, but are not to be dwelled upon or used to stitch up self-determination. To bone up on trickeries, cherry-pick accounts, and to evade reality with the intent of cataloging a fallacy as the truth, files and time are immoral. The risk of falling into a pit that could end in pecuniary delight or socio-politico-economic depression is the question at hand. Whether the fall is intentional or a coincidence, the outcome can be still pondered. On only a few occasions has the spoon of activism weighed more than the barrel of pessimism. When it does happen, the drift of conscientiousness fires the torpid mind and halts the aggression on common sense. In doing so, it takes power away from pictures and words and reinvigorates the value of action.

Nowadays, sophists do not quickly fall into indiscretion or let factual examination downgrade their concept to a dumb claim's level. Whenever a betrayal is uncovered, they bang the revelation with a Machiavellian scheme. We are far from breaking this deceitful trend. One of the numerous reasons is that humans find gratification in these mea culpa parodies, and never hold them accountable for holding a siege on the common-sense bridge. I hope to see the day that obscurantists will publicly be castigated for past mendacity. Lumpen-intellectual claims of expertise is an effort to use credentials to stifle the dialogue required for the betterment of humans. In the painting world, neither the artist nor the canvas has the monopoly of infused delusion. Fanatics and speculators go into it too deeply, and enhance the supernatural scent to a modest riddle. Flirting with misery and shocking contrast around the globe makes it impossible to substantiate certainty. Is it an excuse not to mandate propositions to be plainly explained as the truth?

> "If a liar, who desires to achieve wealth or honours among men,
> needs to use foul means to obtain them, he will say he is con-
> vinced this falsehood was for him a just thing. To those people
> who do not want to search, this action seems to be true,
> and they believe in the liar's strong faith."
>
> —ZERA YACOB

To Arthur Cecil Pigou, Alfred Marshall confessed:

> "(1) Use mathematics as shorthand language, rather than as an en-
> gine of inquiry. (2) Keep to them till you have done. (3) Translate
> into English. (4) Then illustrate by examples that are important in
> real life. (5) Burn the mathematics. (6) If you can't succeed in 4,
> burn 3. This I do often."[1]

At the new crossroad, our conscience is annoyed because the taste of deceitful poison lingers in our throats for a quarter of a lifetime. Demanding to be told the truth can be seen as heroic. The sense of exploit always bleeds dry, then spawns fresh suspicions. A skewed impression is that scholars are anxious to answer burning old questions in their fields, or crack social problems. This myth takes no notice of current trends; research problems

---

1. Marshall and Pigou. *Memorials of Alfred Marshall*, 427.

lie in realm of researchers that survive literature reviews, and could lead to academic advancement (or at least publication in a peer-reviewed journal).

Mathematics' appropriation of social, commerce and trade, and political archipelagos has, as a consequence, the alienation of reasoners and an obsession with reflecting sound thought that aligns with a specific agenda. I cannot understand why any economist would speak with conviction. It is mind-boggling that any blueprint of the future is drafted out of tricks. We come to bet it all, explain it all, and fantasize it all based on probability, which is far different from certainty. Perspicuous characters who bravely charge out of ignorance's trenches were at the mercy of the petty bourgeois and become the target of the nonpareil doctrinaires' hostility and odium.

Mathematical trickeries are based on general chaos without real encounters with a human. Sophists run a regression and do the usual tricks to infer causality, and common sense becomes the culprit. Data, while consistent with an assumption, does not paint the same picture in isolation. It merely justifies believing in theory even after we come into other evidence to the contrary. This emotive option is, in many ways, attractive. The truth derives from sense and reason. It costs a considerable number of neurons to make these two poles mutually accommodating. One of the great ones lost a ton of mazuma gambling in the stock market. He got to face the issue by infusing statistic and probabilities to fulfill economists' egotistical needs. The air of stability cannot last long, and not because of a number. Humans are capricious.

There is a strong assumption of chaos and infinite trends. It is arguably the predominant perspective of most sophists in the economic field today. Matriarchal societies believe that spirit finds a way in a woman's vagina to create the baby; and not a male spermatozoon. We have figured out how this belief is as far from the truth as from the flesh. We have yet to disprove the mystical role in the other part that makes us, us. The oversimplification of phenomena to avoid crossing artificial borders is upsetting. Mortals for whom logic does not exist are mentally clouded and obsessed with one small section of truth. When a considerable number of neurons is wasted picking up clues and trends, we end up in dwarfed senses nebulas.

Our brain processes zillions of options. When asked the color of the sun, the typical off-beam response is red or yellow. Looking for people's intentions, skepticism is available, only to be immediately abused. I turn on scholastic littering like a vengeful fury. It is easier to circle the familiar than to conjure up something new. I asphyxiate when a naïve smile pays homage to old glories that have been proven to be a pile of trash. For creatures who are passive and possess no argument of their own, nonfeasance is the worst of all the wickedness. For better or for worse, I have been cursed with a nefarious and active nosiness: I boastfully take a harder line go seek the truth.

> "It is a shame that education just gives people
> the means to chop logic."
>
> —NATSUME SŌSEKI

Ignorance is bliss; ignorant people are a pain in the ass. Neuter does not mean neutral. For better or worse, every single human is significant to the entire human species, but only knuckleheads make change in the totality of existence. There are two groups whose zealousness makes me puke: morons sailing through the vast sea of poverty and misery for the thrill of it, and primates in expensive suits from renowned tailors on London's legendary Savile Row. The quantity of vile absurdity they absorbed is to blame for their attempt to string up my defiant prose without having a clue about my reasoning. Their second instinct is as draconian as their first: they snake their arms at me to drag me into a parrot fight. I take great pleasure in wasting my life on despicable endeavors. When it comes to dealing with individuals endowed with a considerable common-sense disability, I play dead. Hints of animals' self-awareness or their understanding empathy are well documented. I cook my food and sequester myself to shit; I am human.

The now is tackled by economics' investigators who turn in masses of data, antecedents in peer-reviewed papers, and tabulated statistics; all of which necessitate only some differences of opinion after initial inquiries. In a fairytale in which the economist is portrayed as a savior, it also asserts that community can reign over capitalism's destructive tendencies. Tragedies must tell the beginning, first. The free market is based on a beautiful, colorful badge called efficiency. Efficiency, and not sufficiency, is a better terminology than the real one: waste. We are all a living and breathing contradiction rushing in and piling up wasted in our dual roles as wage earners, depositors, and buyers.

The masters (not you) fear new and blind greed and have kept the entire world from introducing sound commercial doctrine. During the cold war, new concepts could have flourished in non-aligned countries if intellectual dwarves and psychopaths did not fill the movement. It is fatal to claim that clashes between public grievance themes and the elite opulence have been the fuel of socio-politico-economic gimcracks. It is also sinful to argue that in absence of general reaction, moneyers confiscate power from petty bourgeois and the poor. The supremacy of integral signs and equations to smarten a preposterous assumption was not a by-product of the intellectual curiosity of economists and mathematicians. This approach cannot be credited to the public's failure to catch and shame these blasphemers, either. Somehow, it became a part of modern economics because moneyers learned their twisted utility.

Upon the first tackle, you are overawed by packs of feral complexities and confusions over what has become Academicus gunslingers' chief diversions of pulling gaudy models out of their asses. Once melted and dissected well, the whole enchilada becomes disgusting and straightforward. Homo sapiens is tempted to speak fancier as an armament of intellectual authority. The technique of decorating works with mathematical equations and are useful to a minuscule number of readers. Still, dummy variables have yet to demonstrate their rigor or usefulness when the economy falls off a bridge, or social catastrophe occurs. There is more intent in how we do exchange things than a trend; therefore, math is obsolete. For those rascals who yearn for cheap thrills, a rate of interest, commodity prices, security prices, money supplies, and the like are readily available for you to inject into your rotten hearts and heads.

Every academic branch is obsessed with mathematical ornaments, as if creativity is of art, consistency is of science, and the two (creativity and consistency) are mutually exclusive. Beyond dampening creativity, hypothesis interferes with originality and cerebral honesty by pressuring to produce what is expected. The demarcating line between generalizations and stereotypes is washed out. Trashing usual rules of logical argument is not a rejection of knowledge or rationality. Do we need to excommunicate a deeply rooted tradition of how we gain knowledge and learn about things? Not really. Mathematics must take the back seat, where it belongs, just as religion. The arenas of sympathy and the mind need to be engaged in or reoccupied by redrawing the realm of sharing surplus and of "intermerce" (human relation and behavior). The removal of analytical ornaments is imperative for the evolution of social, commerce and trade, and political study.

In a world of flawed understanding and deceptive evidence, there are two crazes in economics. The first is the coloring of people's interactions screenshots. The rationalization for abusing abstract theories powered by mathematical models is that people always intelligently make decisions. Everything is stitched by the belief that we are all self-centered beings who always have something to trade, and get recompensed for what we have to trade. The second is the governments' marketing of interventionist tactics to keep their nations afloat. It is assumed that people are not self-sufficient throughout their life cycle. In most of the developed world, economists favor the former acrobatic to push the latter virtually at the bottom of its trajectory. Economics does not have any superior expertise or knowledge on social dilemmas over other styles of the sermon. The free-market virtuosos had to muster certain persuasive tricks, which got laypeople to pay greater respect to them than to other whizzes making valid arguments from other premises. The smartening of preposterous assumption was not a by-product of intellectual curiosity. It was not achieved accidentally, with the accentuation of global financial crisis.

There is a need for a shift of priorities in conjuring depraved conventions in research or squashing cerebral contraptions. One must smell a real plant and hear the bees to denounce the imaginary patterns abstracting worldviews. Those creatures who bestowed upon themselves the mission of breaking down humanity into an equation ought to face greater scrutiny. The human condition is significantly improved when and where there is a culture to confront social, political, commerce and trade, religious, and cultural propositions. Anarchism got flushed down the toilet the same way as Fascism. Radical intellectuals know that the demise of capitalism is pre-ordained. At no point are they terrified to spontaneously disavow the open display of disillusion and deceit. We have not outgrown the beautification of concepts for the sake of appearance. Right now, it seems impossible to do so. Not everyone is blessed with such audacity: this is one critical aspect of life that the oppressed and depressed all fail to realize.

6

Unfinished Sentences

"You must fear the desperation of the poor and their subsequent revolts. It is always the rich who are attacked by their murderous hands, and often in their fury they make no distinction between the good and the bad."

—OLYMPE DE GOUGES

THE NATURE IS FULL of unusual assemblies and unsatisfactory sounds. The world is a jigsaw puzzle. The awareness of human inclination for diversion calls for a new way of enrolling ourselves in ideals that affect the critical conditions of our existence. Humanity's illnesses have to be presented with pure honesty and an acute psychological understanding. Concepts are born, models triumph, hypothesis vary, and legitimacies mutate. Impregnating the universe with wisdom is a daunting task. Psychedelics assist illiterates in puking out monotonous hypotheses in a counter-intuitive way. Doctrines generate a chromatic emotional state in poets far more conflicting than in fiends bent on global evildoing.

The Victorian era's scholars were forward-thinking concerning the body of their probes. They were not enthralled by the venture of challenging social pyramids. Their fights for the individual's right of conscience to resolve the accumulated flaws of feudal society lacked the depth to evict mystical beings and incoherence purportedly from their world. A selection of their pieces sliced through their generation's serene pessimisms with disturbing eloquence. Their works, which are still revered to this day, do not tackle the specific political events of the era: all expose the twisted favoritisms of their time.

The anti-capitalism movements were rich in exceptional personalities and gusty ideas. Supporters of political economy theories and skeptics started to pin down the startling link between obsession and confusion. The counter-elites cracked patterns and encryptions that were hidden in political economy psalms which started to deflate mysticism's influence on the public. There were apostles of the gradual dialectic, the Hegelian's views, who were sure and certain that history was a slow and steady unfolding of human mandate. The libertarian anarchists declared that all property was theft and sought to disarticulate every joint of the state. The utopian socialist advocated collective ownership of the means of production. The communists fought for the creation of commune or worker cooperatives. Frenetic discussions and writings altered our hyperawareness in more ways than one. Revolutionaries depicted the church and the state to be a single corrupt institution which does not act in the best interests of the people. The uncompromising thinkers vowed to pinpoint the forces controlling our sentiments and figure out what makes us human. Little was out of bounds. The analytical assaults on injustice's phlegm and the call for reason in the place of revelation went on to spark rage, in following centuries, in free thinkers all over the globe.

The merit of living in a fast-evolving world is that it always contests the resettlement of ideals, from the encephalon into the existent. Idyllic colonists and ruling classes across Europe were shaken by gruesome spectacles of the slaves and the poor, pounding mansions gates raucously, demanding individual liberty and equality. Fearing the spread of radical ideas, European governments responded by prosecuting hell-raisers for seditious libel and treason. Colonial rulers responded without mercy. They razed entire cities to the ground. By and large, the uprisings' glitch is in the intelligent factions' failure to overcome prudence at the right time. Sniffing the results of their anger, one is left to wonder if this period is a parody of overcoming. It failed to become the age of reason.

The bourgeois' robust determination to keep the cliques excluded from the networks of power, from taking the lead to saving the people from exploitation, is not without merit. The faction of a rebellion which is the fiercest and the most responsive to change, or adaptive to the environment, wins it all. The moderate voices' reluctance to be the central part of a theatrical effort prompts ruthless buccaneers to ascend and cleverly bend social dialogue to further their agenda. The smoldered social fairness and public eagerness for drastic changes gives them a giant canvas to splatter on, philosophically. There are a lot of instances when comrades sentenced God to death in their efforts to become divine humans. While God jerked up on the rope, radical thinkers turned society upside down and bloody.

The Jacobins were not the last group to be in a war of extermination. They laid in wait on the steps of the palaces and stabbed the owners as they come out. They then proceeded to annihilate their friends and foes. Successful socialist and communist movements have had an intense dislike of dissent. The Bolsheviks used the spontaneous intersection of their thoughts and exposed a hidden face of nature's exquisite beauty to seduce the masses. Their power and vision swelled, as did their apparatus of viciousness. The fact that there are so few characters of color among economics halls of fame inductees doesn't mean the social, commerce and trade, and political madhouse is not racially diverse. In Cuba, Fidel Castro latched onto the Soviets under the pretext of seeking assistance in installing a participative culture in which people's voices count regardless of their race or background. He summarily executed the cliques he dethroned, which was celebrated. The dictatorship of the proletariat violently crushed the oppressors, the exploiters, and the capitalists just as they did to their colleagues' defiance. In most minds, the bones of millions of Cambodians are a macabre confirmation that the pre-eminent dispute of our age, collectivism versus individualism, has been settled.

The shepherds and their sheep-like mindsets, twisted in impossibilism and stagism to permanent revolution, led to the death of millions in revolution and counter-insurrections. None of the labor-centric movement philosophers and suzerains ever did manual labor for a living or managed any enterprise. The hardest thing that they did manually before these socioeconomic grisly tryouts was writing tracts which announced their ideological dedication. The Victorian succubus' incomplete hypnotic sermons lured unknowing dupes and psychopaths onto the same dance floor. The suspicion that the whole capitalistic culture is moving toward a catastrophe still subjugates millions to tyrannies; for social justice impersonators have gone too far to preserve their political power, and the abolition of private property has been labeled as silly and irrational. Atrocities committed under the Marxist banner has automatically made capitalism the right fit for humanity. The mere thought of switching from the market economy to any new scheme has become a crime.

Unfinished Sentences

"Under capitalism, man exploits man. Under communism, it's
just the opposite."

—JOHN KENNETH GALBRAITH

Priceless neurons and time have been squandered in the effort to sort
out if poverty is capitalism polydactyly, or the consequence of communism's
theoretical oligodactyly. Some conducted an esophagogastroduodenoscopy
on nations to understand wealth and saw an amenable arrangement in wages.
Utopian thinkers have always been regarded as Don Quixotes or belletrists
by antiheroes who argue that allocating resources based on need or equality
is not fair. They sought to root out "all the evils of a society" by outlawing arrangements between individuals. Is there a clear emotional difference when
society chooses not make any person worse off, and no person should be
injured by choices made by the group? Alternatively, what about when each
person is responsible for their future no matter what happens?

The twentieth-century sunk the distributive justice discourse in
an abyss of ignorance. Eugenics made the gap in reason and philosophy,
where both logical arrangement and pretexted every human problem,
nonexistent. It could well be defined by crusades to annihilate premises
contradictory to the tenets of neoclassical economic theory. A social blueprint that competes with free-marketers' templates was hastily dismissed.
Where capitalistic views reigned supreme, the imaginary link between the
betterment of the poor and the commerce and trade crisis became a fact.
Lumpen-intelletuals enthusiastically endorsed corporate parasitic behaviors. They have fine-tuned the free-for-all slogan by muddling together
monetarist amnesia and developmental schizophrenia with a dash of op-
portunist pragmatism. Money-grubbing was elevated to the noble rank of
a divine quest. Intimidation tactics were masked as economic policies. A
heavy emphasis was given to the defense of property rights.

Sputnik One's echoes created new symbols and new jingles all over the
world. Communists attacked capitalist creeds, indicting clerics and bourgeois for their lust for power and wealth. The surreptitious defenders of
the established power structure were portrayed as gurus for their conniv-
ing response to social injustice. They presented the history of capitalism as
one of exploitation and debauchery. Communities in which members put
the means of production into collective decision-making structures should
also be held responsible for the degree of deliberate slayings of large groups
of people to amass minimum long-term profits. Communist stances led to
a descent into contradictions under the real-world conditions of continual

change. Karl Marx had, in a dialectical, materialistic way, admitted the necessity of the bourgeoisie's egoism for social progress. More than a century
after the death of Marx, Trường Chinh, a leader of the Communist Party of
Vietnam, agreed with him. These concessions attribute a sense of benevolence to the capitalist animal spirit in an eerie way.

Labor unions are nothing more than a capitalist ulnar hexadactyly.
Capitalism did tremendously curtail the ancient power of worker confrater-
nities on commerce and trade. Trade unions were the legacy of the guilds'
sentiment by which the workers combatted and lessened their exploitation.
At first, they kicked the new machinery with sabots. Gradually, the workers
came to realize the value of coalescing when bargaining with their employ-
ers to obtain a better rate for their muscles. At first glance, this expression
of rational self-interest seems to have socialistic attributes. It turns out that
the effort is in fact very capitalistic; an appendage of capitalism.

Here comes Vishnugupt's central question: "Of a rascal and a serpent,
the serpent is the better of the two, for he strikes only at the time he is
destined to kill, while the former at every step." The answer is never permanent. Pals who look for answers past science and common sense end up
falling in love with fools and foolishness. Protestors talk about the social
malaise without pointing out the rights and wrongs or what caused them.
Souls sympathizing with communism should tour North Korea. Capitalists
are becoming quite critical of the free market. Everywhere on this perplexing panorama, sages are in a long pursuit in the same direction to exter-
minate their ideological foes. The resistance's antiphons to maintain what
mostly is a wall of privilege and tradition is chanted by oppressors as well
as the oppressed. We fail to realize that capitalism and communism are
in fact Siamese monstrosities, rejecting their respective premises without
acknowledging the need for the meaning it provides.

> "I don't think whether you believe in capitalism, or you believe in
> communism or socialism. I think nobody can dispute that
> [it is right] to fight for a just and equal society."
>
> —ONG BOON HUA

Conscious reasoning's process is not unique to homo sapiens; other
creatures do hesitate before making a sound or doing something. There are
few elements and compounds of which only humans are made. The ability
to devise an excuse for a personal act of pure evil seems to be one of them.
Why ordinary human beings conspire to organize themselves into trading

other human beings, is undoubtedly the most intriguing question we can ask. In the appraisal of a contentious social arrangement, dogmatism and condescension are anesthetizing. Nothing limits humans' pursuit of phenomena that are improbably well-balanced. This is the principle behind lotteries, dating, and religion. Looking closely at our most fêted fictitious triumphs, their metamorphosis seems unlikely, for remembrance. The very first memories we have of our existence hardly sketched out the territory of the things we became fanatical about. Our investment in disputing what determines our viewpoints and made and unmade us neglects to address indispensable blunders and desperate paradoxes.

Why haven't we become humans? Satanists are a lot more interested in what they see as community activism and individual freedoms than in performing bizarre rites. The events that plagued the minds of Europeans in the twentieth-century facilitated Communism, Nazism, Fascism, Nationalism, Imperialism, and other reckless creeds to make their way across the globe. The very early miscarriages of social justice induced by the deities made Europe more vulnerable to devastating events. Moguls and monarchs hired conformists who exhibited a considerable degree of intellect or secret knowledge to violate natural laws. Socioeconomic wrongs have been around for a very long time. Prior centuries' Übermenschen were shrewd analysts of these paradigm shifts, but awful forecaster of human emancipation. Their contentious ways of projecting the creation and existence crescendos tricked science and art concessions alike. But the flares of social dissensions were incited by slaves of different gender and ages, who yearned to become men, with the machismo and ignorance that this entails. No one sought to become human. The universe hardly dispenses to skeptics an idea more effective than a psychosomatically buffed alibi. It is perhaps an act of mercy.

> "I am tired of talk that comes to nothing. It makes my heart sick when I remember all the good words and all the broken promises. There has been too much talking by men who had no right to talk."
>
> —HIN-MAH-TOO-YAH-LAT-KEKT,
> HINMATÓOWYALAHTQ'IT

When Spanish colonists lashed out against Friar Bartolomé De las Casas for advocating the Native American right to freedom, he labeled the negroes as a far better alternative for menial labor. The Catholic church agreed. The history of the shitty hole from where I began to lug my humanism has been one of grandiose repressions, exploitations, and civil wars. I have been entrenched in that reality since birth. My peregrination has been inundated with depressed zombies' rotten hands. These lenses help me notice different shapes and colors of socioeconomic injustices. I have no qualms about denouncing the nauseating culture that dehumanizes the deprived, raids a vulnerable social caste, or promotes coldness toward the destitute because I have been knocked out by poverty's ricochets, and not just once. The most ubiquitous challenge humanity faces is from scheming, non-exploitative human relationships alongside resource distribution and expansion symbiosis.

Yoking peasants and the weak was, for a long time in history, the elite, God-given responsibility and duty of preserving social order. To meet their fiduciary obligation of funding their shareholders' obsessive opulence, conglomerates routinely slash the quality of goods and services to siphon the most money out of all of us. One has to tenaciously fight the urge to pile stacks of blame on moneyers to sort out the tone of sorites' paradoxes. The flood of chocolate bars in all shapes and forms at a green party's congress peels off a noble intent from the members and contributors' gallantry. The gangs of social justice impersonators approach and proposition such, as co-ops are doing nothing more than defusing real radical socio-economic changes.

There is an absolute consensus around the need for new social, commerce and trade, and coherent political concepts. Cooperatives and cap-and-trade, or the refurbished community marketplace and means of transport as a new economy, and gentler strategies of stockpiling wealth, are gaining momentum. These enthusing actions countersigning are pranks. The modern trope misstates how and why sane minds could act wantonly when it comes to enslaving other beings and to accumulating stuff. The symptoms are maladies manifested, not indicative of the disease's causes. The scapegoating of cheap goods and services and the proliferation of piggishness conceals the absolute magnitude of global social, commerce and trade, and political fissures.

The absence of intoxicating substitutes to ecumenical singing providing meaning to animate existence caused an existential dread. The terror of objecting to Deus Vult kept collective moral sense from adventuring on the other side of misery. The ridiculous fear of generating a philosophical vacuum overshadows the critical context of truth's expiration. We request a substitute before letting go of evil. Thomas Paine's ideological progenies, led by Lucifer, broke ranks with the self-determination campaigners and stormed the dungeon where God was held, and a pitched battle erupted. By the time it was over, they had freed the recidivists and beheaded the ideas of equality and human and civil rights. As a sign of gratitude, God aided the victors in the suppression of Allah's power over human bondage and provided ruses to prolong European moral decay.

"Make up your mind, Snail! You are half inside your house,
and halfway out."

—RICHARD NATHANIEL WRIGHT

The decline of phobias inherited from past centuries is not the one causing bedlam in the third world. The fundamentals of colonial economics involved exporting unprocessed raw materials and levying colonial taxes for the benefit of the metropolis. Local communities had no say in the extraction of resources. A skimpy investment was made into indigenous social welfare, such as an education fitted perfectly for a subhuman. Former European colonies ought to tip their hats to Germany, as it has been framed as the initiator of both giant clashes of civilizations. During the world wars of the twentieth-century, great European empires had to break all sorts of taboos, from racial to spiritual, for their national survival. They poured troops from their gardens onto the killing fields and ordered lower-grade races to kill white supermen. The psychological precursors of events are leading up to the vanguard of the oppressed audacious petitions for the right to self-govern. The masters who fought to retain their liberty, which provided the basis for the Western world, did not tolerate their colonies' demands for greater self-government using the same basis. Independence movements were met with severe repression, and some of their leaders even paid the extreme penalty at the gallows, while many were jailed.

A rebellion is far from evidence of a vibrant, intelligent culture amongst the oppressed. When former colonies gained control of the means to which they have not previously had access, they embraced the former masters' commerce and trade policies with little scrutiny. They climbed back up their huge curves into the same Victorian corsets. The adopted commercial system-based colonization's extrinsic notion of Martial Races and Les Races Guerrières, and social welfare generated what their politicians saw as a pile of unmarked funds, easy for them to misappropriate. Their freshly molded ruling classes awarded themselves the entitlement of a lifestyle underwritten by an extended set of variations of human bondage. The principle of wealth has to be gotten and preserved through *Septem*

Peccata Mortalia, but did not preclude some members of the elite from being victimized by the privilege they practiced.

During the cold war, new concepts could not flourish in non-aligned countries even if the movement was filled by all the scholars of that time. Communism and socialism's moralities stirred devotion of gullible third world national heroes. It also increased the appetites of caimans. The nascent nations' elites, spitting out picturesque verses, were ominous signs of mental disquietude. Their head honcho submerged their megalomaniacal sense of their own destiny in guiding principles. Not long after, the relationship between the elite and the masses turned sour. A glimpse of non-aligned nations' rapacious attitudes toward harmless and kindhearted souls bathed in an ocean of delusional unconscientiousness kept every darker corner of the world in the dark—or should I be kind and say, at least in part. The inherent colonial brutality has led this block to another genre of never-ending social, commerce and trade, and political genocides.

The dialogues among developing nations' leprechauns are framed by their narrow-minded insistence on traditional doctrines imported from the west. In these parts of the world, higher learning centers are regularly refilled with adherents of various orders for whom philosophical sources are in isolation from their social contexts. The status of aficionado is solely granted through absolute obedience to racist sages from the better-off side of the globe. To conserve or to enhance this prestige, the academic dons eagerly circulate outdated concepts and systems of belief which are manufactured based the colonial portrait of indigenous peoples as barbarians alongside European efforts to seize native lands. The injustices deeply entrenched in their fallacious "truth" continued to be aired unabated throughout the twentieth century. Foreign felons and conglomerates wielding great influence on a myopic and extremely rapacious gang calling the shots on wobbling nations' internal affairs is one sign of the indigenous off-center acuity. For homegrown moralists, it one thing to be discounted in history by colonizers, but it is quite another when people with whom they have a great deal in common fail to consider their unflinching tone in local or global discourses. The message is that only Caucasians' verdicts count.

Crusaders with the intention of saving shitty parts of the world rely on their privilege to devise social maneuvers. Do-gooders immerse themselves in sophisticated speculation about the origins of developing nations' despair without acknowledging the agony in their own back yard. They are concerned with making and implementing injustices according to fair processes. Their view's lopsidedness is the result of the strong inclination of their minds to depreciate other cultures. Their ignorance of historical reality, particularly anything outside of a small geographical bubble which social justice movements claim to transform, is the most significant weakness of all.

Even while losing legitimacy in the eyes and hearts of the growing legions of the disoriented, the free market is still managing to keep the whole predator-prey convention appear sustainable. We have all lost the pure taste of life's happiness. One could assume that the socio-economic symptoms exhibited make visible what needs to be done. There is a dark constellation of pretext faltering on social justice. We are still buying into roles assigned to social classes in the eighteenth-century libretto, as if time intervals set the recurrence of experiences. The acquiescence of the capitalistic working class is inherited from the properties of mercantilism's prejudice and thralldom. Hustling day in and day out yet still being rooted in poverty causes wisdom's shrinkage and involuntary spasms of anger. Meditation would cool off the self-enslaved, but it is not a cure for the moral and physical condition. The social and political ecosystem does matter.

The heterodoxy economics maharishis and their disciples' failure to adequately address developed nations' losing streaks is making financial crisis a normal condition of global commerce and trade. The modern commerce and trade melodies are set to two esculent rhythms: continue patching capitalism, and resuscitate communism. The first option is what we have now: moneyers are leading us off the cliff. The second option of enduring waves of sadism is being snubbed, contested, and rejected. The world should be heading for the third option, and thinking about something new. However, it is not! While in the Western hemisphere solons are pleasuring each other behind academic barrack walls, the rest of the world is avoiding facing the unpleasant truth: we ought to trash the whole system and try something new, on our own. We do not know where to start.

> "Writing isn't an easy taskmaster. Sentences left unfinished never continue as well as they had begun. New ideas bend the main arch of the text, and it never again sits perfectly true."
>
> —MAGDA SZABÓ

Primitive scholasticism had the only unworldly excuse for phenomena. Almost without exception, motions were dictated by deities. Social constructs do turn passion into nothing more than a test of mores.

Psychological contracts are to blame for the spillover of corrosive doctrines into the domain of wisdom, or for the intelligentsia's vileness. Distressed areas pump out sounds audible from a distance. Agony traps an entire society in a long period of irrational behaviors. When the right combination of organized noises and scallywags is added into the loop, dogmas take precedence to logic for defusing blight and injustice. The aggregated memoir of humanity offers a fuzzy way out. Theoreticians make us all fall in love with extensions of rusty claims. Mantras crafted from turds have been shifting the jurisdiction of human fate between doctrines and mysticism. The initial stage and ambiance do matter in grasping the nuance and tone of long-lasting rituals.

A particular set of circumstances is required in order for reality to rend the vindictiveness from the intellectual. Most overconfident idealists' spin on the future of humanity is a condensed form of their eccentricity. Exceptional personages who possess paradigm-shifting flair have traditionally been part of revolutionary platforms. They make the most profound changes of the human condition, for better or worse, by observing attentively someone else's pain or joy, typically over a period of time. Some dissenters seem to have a series of lifetimes harassing society's cataleptic states of hypnotism. Their full commitment to awakening humans' inherent attributes, being responsible for the decisions made individually or as a herd, is praiseworthy.

"Was ist Aufklärung"? This is the age of edgy inquiries only on taboos that white men have opted to confront. The scientific achievements of the Victorian era glossed over the idea of a universe that was governed by physical laws and not by divine providence. Nature's myths were discredited, one after another, faster than ever before. Reasoning gained substantial grounds in the mind and spirit of the ordinary mortal. Impulsive novelists, critics, and poets scrubbed the baseline of what it means to be human. When it came to gender, slavery, and imperialism, nearly all of them delved deep into the supernatural to exonerate idiosyncrasies. Nothing worth heartburn was being concocted on injustice in other parts of the world around the same epoch: this is is a grotesque claim. Other societies implanted slave trading schemes centuries before European explorers, conquistadores, and missionaries arrived. Lector priests did not put brobdingnagian effort into rationalizing the horrifying sybaritism that the elite enjoyed.

Theories do not reveal the dynamics underlying this philosophic shift. The fundamental postulate of economics, that incentives influence human behavior, is not concerned with whether it is possible to assess the consequences of the verdict appropriately. Heterodox economists who attempt to raise rationality to the status of moral principle display flashing rhetoric. It takes time before they get wrapped up in their anger and completely flip out. When that happens, they go into screaming rages and continue to rant the same things over and over again. The malcontents' childish comportments embolden free-marketers to prowl around like roaring beasts looking for someone to devour. Fear-provoking radical ideas that threaten prime factors of social injustice with monotone variations end up having a little impact on the universe. Hang-ups will always fail to invalidate the kind of delicately calibrated misconceptions which had given economists prestige and purpose.

Since the industrial revolution, one wrong, slavery, has been replaced (or at least matched) by another: indigence. We are unanimous in demolishing poverty. When it comes to how to do it, the cultural acceptability of inequality is deemed as being necessary for all, to usher in a better course of human evolution. The desire of imposing a mechanism for a decent universal standard of living is so passé. Artificial traumas keep decent folks on the outskirts of bringing positive thoughts to life. The common substrate has remained the same throughout human history in disoriented minds. Political economy has become a sinkhole of thoughts and passion. Idiocy and prejudice hybrids feed upon academia in some recursive, synthesized experiences. Each generation goes further, in sophisticating the madness, than the generations preceding it. Historically predominant radical voices would have gotten a better deal in history books if they did not grab some z's or resort to jumping in a hydrotherapy pool at the peak of their fury eruptions.

> "Do not seek to follow in the footsteps of the wise.
> Seek what they sought."
>
> —MATSUO CHŪEMON MUNEFUSA

Why don't current social, commerce and trade, and political torments spring out dissensions in the laboring ranks, instead of a full-blown class conflict? Dangerous ambitions and fascinations brought the world as we know it into being very obscure. In Greek mythology, Sisyphus was sentenced, for his deceits, to roll a huge rock up a hill, only to watch it roll faster down the hill, to repeat this laborious and futile exploit for eternity. A debate about criteria for allocating compassion has irritated dreamers and truth-seekers since humans decided to be infinite. As the supernatural ceased to be the source of principles and criteria to determine how resources should be divided among people, superhuman beings sought to decrypt the complex forces that governed everyday lives. They speculated and contested whether principles such as need, equality, compensation, and contribution are independent of one another or could be combined. It is comforting to think of the influential theorists of the time as imposing figures staring sternly back at us. Their quixotic pursuit drove their bodies into poignant seclusion and their minds into overindulgences. We come to think of bravura as giving people the excuse to individually craft their meaning of life.

It is hard for most to articulate; to express innermost feelings using the proper terms. Bringing bold ideas into the spotlight without trying to understand what sparked hallucinations in the context of space and time diffuses theorists' insecurities, and personal tragedies are completely ludicrous. But that is what my contemporary does all the time. A good listener pays attention to an interlocutor's words and demeanor, time and space, and his voice's variating tone to capture what people mean rather than say. The root cause of past indignations is still here with us, making the daunting objective achievable. Global melancholy offers us a reason and compassion exposes a way out. A coveted academic badge is the proper excuse to shut down empathy towards the less fortunate. Whereas some see themselves as heroes; for the masters, they are simply useful types. Even as we become more compassionate beings, individualism's ideological rewards keep our focus on our self-examination.

We do not see our shadows when we look at ourselves in the mirror. The cradle of our collective conscience lies in human fixations over ecstatically guesstimating imminent possibilities. This disposition confines thoughts to a place where it is hard to muster compassion for words in the shadow of prejudices and humiliations. The reputation of neoclassical economics has somewhat declined. Real-world realities have been interfering in the orderly process of the entire economic field of recognition and anointment. Regimes no longer need to conjure up a divine right to be legitimate. Coherent concepts emerge without reference to God. The opium of the people, as Marx called religion, lost it potency through the widespread desire to better understand us. To work up vague approval for enlightening abnormality, we stubbornly extract from our incubuses the instantiated ideals to deepen the competence of our phantasms. Moreover, this mania is prolonged by the desire to immortalize every flare of brilliance.

More than ever before, the northeastern hemisphere is today overdeveloped with primitive emotions, and the rest of the world is the opposite. Third world obsequiousness has continually reinforced the primacy of the free market. Depressing streets across the southern hemisphere have been portrayed as the consequence of grandiose despotism, exploitation, and civil wars. Western neoclassical practitioners have never been held accountable for the reforms shoved down dark countries' throats. These white men, women, and teenagers continue using former colonies as a testing ground for ideas that are too radical to be applied at home. Contrary to the popular beliefs of modern Tirailleurs Indochinois and Tirailleurs Senegalais, socioeconomic expansion does not translate to peace. If we can learn something from WWI and WWII, African nations' civil wars, commotions in each corner of the East, and racism, it's that peace succumbs to socioeconomic caprices or fiascoes.

The coral reefs bleaching, the Mara Salvatrucha campaigns of terror in the Northern Triangle, Abakua, and the Great Chinese Famine are all consequences of social, commerce and trace, and political scintillation's flaws. What the point of talking about saving the ecosystem without taking on social justice? Solidarity wagers approached the root of injustices in a very candid way. The association of the term 'anarchy' with chaos has made the absence of authority our collective phobia. History shows that border walls keep only the poor apart, and trade agreements strengthen the grip of the rich on commerce and trade interfaces. Prior centuries' social, commerce and trade, and political principles (like Marxists' catechism), in their theoretical frames, have gotten part of the way. Considerable challenges must be faced in attempting to reconstruct plausible interpretations of longstanding systems of thought to remain cognizant of the dangers inherent in using current reality to understand old attitudes. Canvassers ought to take an inductive approach to stabbing deep into the capillaries of the current hidden state.

By the mid-twenty-first century, there was a renewed, growing, skeptical attitude toward capitalism's accepted premises. It was an incredibly fascinating time in history for the voyeurs and other mediocre beings who enjoy sudden gusts of human collective anguish. Distributive justice explorers, individuals, sought to alter the human experience positively and to stop conflating inequality and poverty. Then, capitalist propagandists incorporated the newest fables and the most up-to-date trickeries to prevent and mitigate ideological mutiny risks. The challenge for a prosecutor to convince cynics and the panicky jury was not in the closing argument's potency. Militants have been misled by other dogma's emotional appeal and have lost the case for ending capitalism because of their premature urges.

As we are all interconnected, dignity shouldn't lose significance. There has been a lot of economic and philosophical redundancy in the attempt to fabricate a substitute complementary to capitalism. Setting out to critique and to attack the current malaise achieves nothing good. When people are agonizing, they end up trying to organize noises instead of paying attention to the signal. This is when emotions take precedence over logic and disarticulate social justice's reasonable argument. Free-marketer nemeses have been actively seeking to affect a critical shift. There is a small variation in voices railing against social, commerce and trade, and political injustice. They have struggled with the question of wealth and justice and continue to come up short. They do not bring anything new or of significance to the table other than beautiful tables and colorful charts. Their misfires intensify the noises. The invalidation of emotions has only led to a fatal reassurance that all the locks and bolts look alike, at the right place.

In a society in which Machiavellian methods to get rich or to tighten social order are regarded as assisting in the betterment of the only surviving species of the genus homo (or a contribution to the union), any real social justice experiment is doomed. Adventurers' continuous efforts to achieve intellectual honesty to bring a total revolution (rather than just reform) ought to dive into our collective unconscious. We have traded our need for a bunch of things for our want of bunch of stuff. We sacrifice for our demise by stultifying the petition for a dignified life. Everything tastes like chicken—or, simply put, like nothing: we do not even remember what chicken tastes like.

An anti-capitalism conviction cannot be overturned without acute eyesight. Social context does matter in grasping the nuance and tone of long-lasting traditions. The most critical and exploited resource in the twenty-first century is human creativity. It is, at the same time, extemporaneous and infinite. An unfinished sentence can be revitalized to cripple the specter haunting the world.

Penitence!!!

Today you again smiled purely,
And said that you have overfilled the production plan threefold,
But I do not envy your achievement,
I can do even better,
But I like your smile.
Why is it so pure?

—CHO KI-CHON

Social innovations and trade reamendments have failed to bridge the gap between the deplorable what is and the incredible what ought to be.

7

Tragic Love Story

"The aspirations of colonized and enslave peoples
are everywhere the same; their lot too is the same."

—PATRICE EMERY LUMUMBA

DID HUMANS CREATE AHURA Mazda, or did God create humans? The answer matters only to pathetic creatures. The oldest part of Jerusalem is a mirror depicting the central delusion of our times. Dividing quarters by religion to strictly preserve invalid boundaries and laws creates worlds that are so close and yet so far apart from each other. From here, radical stands that stem from religious and secular fallacies have closed, for everyone, the sense of humor and common-sense corridors and opened the golden gate of egocentrism and intolerance. Tiptoeing across all demarcating lines in Old Jerusalem crushes the logic of what billions of souls have been kneeling to.

Poverty triggers confusion and the loss of mental activity. Hardship paralyzes the ability to sort out presumptions and illusions. Labeling the other holds a controversial history, for vulnerable populations. Social disfigurement makes emotions' stimulus disappear into shadow and motivates cynicism until the poor's compassion towards other poor people gradually declines into apathy. The Dajabón River is just another museum full of chef d'oeuvres made by the poor with other poor people's blood. Losers of the birth lottery teleported into the land of hope and glory, in which they can be anything they want to be, generally hold to their initial nauseating social construct and spiritual phantasm.

It is indeed disheartening that white people in Butte, Montana, in the US, think that they are better off than brownies in Potosi Bolivia. The gangs of the oppressed are sadistically seizing every opportunity on the poverty tourism sector to turn millions of people's excruciating and humiliating socioeconomic and health realities into a pile of cash. The universal peccancy of hominids is full of vectors pointing in every possible direction. The predominance of disgraceful dots in society's development backstory attests to moral decay's persistence. The whimsical collective conscience grants leniency to those who are accomplices of nefarious maneuvers greater than petty theft. Thus, just as through certain drugs or religion make humans stupid and insane, men are rendered dull and stolid by capitalistic delusions.

All over Sadr City in Bagdad, Iraq, misery has an unusual aroma and tenor; more so than in Strawberry Mansion, Philadelphia, USA. A ridiculous amount of energy might build an appreciable improvement in the stock of the shabby ideals of liberty, equality, and fraternity. Solidarity will remain inert or full of bungling performances until thoughts attaching prime importance to humans are nurtured. Inequality is proclaimed a buttress against social collapse by the marginalized and the lunatic fringe of the wealthy. Murmurs of inequality do not capture much of the public's attention, as the ones harmed by injustice are consistently and diligently tearing each other apart.

In Medieval Europe, much of the coercive power of the aristocracy weakened. The attitudes inherited from the feudal order did not substantially shift. An insurrection is far from evidence of vibrant, intelligent culture amongst the oppressed. When former colonies gained the control of means to which they had not previously had access, their freshly molded ruling classes awarded themselves the entitlement of a lifestyle underwritten by an extended set of variations of human bondage. Eunuch scholars' smirks nullify the effects indicating that injustice is the chief culprit of poverty. In a pocket of anti-capitalism resistance, the elite imposes flimsy restrictions on moneyers while crushing proletariat ideals. The poor are aware of this social and political inequality, but perceive their position as natural.

You may also notice that, after making a little bit of money, people of at the bottom of the social and political pyramid become light-hearted, joyous, and inclined to dance and sing. A small amount of money has great power to make a chaste person lascivious or a shy individual confident by merely deforming a particular viewpoint of the lifecycle. Such is the beautiful secret of capitalism, though, of course, it is concealed under a pile of fallacies. Exquisiteness, poverty, malice, and coldness are all multifaceted.

The savage civilizations are said to be hostile to justice even as they are ignorant of it. It is doubtful that this forged consideration may not one day be in high request, especially when we consider its broad utility for conglomerations and the innumerable poverty which anger brings upon the poor. The poor are infatuated with modern dominant commerce and trade creeds. Generally, the ones at the bottom know little of the social, commerce and trade, and political arrangement apogee. They also don't believe that the free market can do anything but keep them poor. There is no more significant cause of death than despair.

Where narcissism and selfishness are the most esteemed traits, and a strong hand is admired, the themes of debates have no ingredient other than obedience and politics. After dissecting the perception of distributive justice and procedural justice and their relationship with the machine of the twenty-first century despotic regimes, one can deduce that there aren't any dictators left. Dictatorship has been replaced by immature Caesarism: a system in which each of the dominators and those suffocated stand to their role and rank and respects the script. Allegiance and moral delinquency are related to spirituous fantasies and ethnic or class membership. The vassals would simply refuse to admit the failure of their lords, whom they blindly support to the grave. Alas, the devotion to folly takes precedence over the collective national interest of social progress. Often, when one of the vassals is out of arguments that he is there to convince with the persistence of his vis-a-vis, insults become the preferred weapon of destabilization.

> "Why is something that builds up humans through commerce
> and trade now destroying humanity?"
>
> —GEORGE WASHINGTON CARVER

Capitalism made humanity into daydreamers and gilded the worst in a human until the truth all but vanished. It has locked in a fatal embrace between social benefit and the ecosystem's demise, activism and radicalism, and aspirations and trauma. Maddening condescension has generated more alms for the poor than all the virtues together. Serfs and slaves fought their way to self-determination from landowners. Lumpen-intellectuals endorse moneyers' boorish avarice and the impoverished materialism, enthuse third world adolescents, and are subsidized by the rich states. The modern world's prominent melody, chanted out of the mystical corridor to the cornucopia, depicts social welfare as a burden on solely the rich. Poverty's physical and psychological brutality has yet to put to the test our bonds of loyalty to spiritual creeds.

Humanity has devised multi-layer fantasies to deal with social injustices. The concoctions of religious ruses and scientific methods have become more refined with impressive cerebral ornaments. Deified lumpen-intellectuals, politicians, and clergymen dazzle us with quixotic solutions to social plights. The public pulls out revolvers and begins blasting away self-professed liberators and protectors who accidentally reveal their clay feet. Why has no civilization protested against the general state of intellectualism and spirituality at the same time? The global double standard critics do not adequately point out the source of hypocrisy and prejudice.

Why are we miserable? Our default mode is to ruminate excessively on autobiographical stories. Graphs are becoming insidious acts of transgression. We are probably no longer convinced by the tales of old narratives that portrayed social injustices as natural disasters. Humanity's self-portraits depict widespread isolation and despair. We feel trapped in an empty frame. Humankind's emotions have been chopped off, and everything we would usually use to make contact with the outside world has been taken away. Capitalism is plunging us into an unsettling world. Behind the facade of competition and capitalism's anthem, except for a few of us, we are all vulnerable and abandoned. Some minds have captured the global restless, angst-ridden mood. The global computer network is providing a variety of information and makes it difficult to deny that the entire world is in the midst of a crisis.

Social injustice inquiries or dialogue about ethical, social constructs of power and privilege is onerous. The challenge lies in getting closer to what it is and how it is perceived by the those who are experiencing it. Esotericism of mainstream economics has made socioeconomic inquiry, interpretation, and explanation mainly of a hermeneutic nature. In the study of people in the shittiest parts of the globe, there is little or no attempt to make sense of misery and despair regarding the meaning of people who experience it. The crux of anthropologic and sociological canvassers' aims lies in looking for the generalizability of findings to apply to a larger group of people. Western scholastic arrogance and Eastern dedication to a super-human controlling power freeze a torrent of consciousness when dealing with dilapidated parts of the world.

Demystifying causes of social injustices is the noblest endeavor that one can undertake, yet is the most deserted turf, as well. Creativity transcends cultural boundaries not metaphorically, but in real terms. We are wasting time and energy attempting to disentangle capitalism as a misnomer while capitalism the monster is shoving baloney down our throats. The current patterns of life are far different from the English social and political context of the Victorian world. Genetically, we have not changed much. Epigenetically? That is another story.

Capitalism is long past its prime. The kernel of capitalism lies in mass productivity-based human despair, not mass creativity or sustainability. The barbaric commerce and trade arrangement still is the most dynamic method for coercion of the will and common sense's asphyxiation, which has no relevance in recent existence. While it has maintained an endurable, mortifying linearity for the common standard of living, recent financial and media instruments have made it possible for culprits to grow their wealth and spheres of influence exponentially. Nothing is more remarkable than the anxiety of a genesis. Alas, the story of capitalism produces only greater heat than anger.

> "It seems that the inevitable fate of man is never to attain complete freedom: princes everywhere tend to despotism and the people to servitude."
>
> —JEAN-PAUL MARAT

Life is about living by taking refuge in the study of the hidden secrets of nature, not by means of books. After devoting the best part of an existence diving into the worst part of what different civilizations have to offer, and in the company of shrewd beings and judicious dons, I arrived at this melancholic conclusion: the hearts of superhumans are set either on narcissistic schemes or on the accumulation of wealth by any and all means. The more one drinks from the immense fount of knowledge, the more painfully thirst increases. One has to deny the very existence of the cure for the irresistible longing to become possessed, at least once in our lifetime, by compassion. In the same way, opiates are not remedies for improving the general conditions of mediocre minds or preventing the ascent of hatred to privileged brains.

Countless questions are not understood, but are thought to be passably solved. Eighteenth-century sages deplored régimes' interference, enabled by wrong-headed dogmas. It was an asymptote. The Edict of Nantes recognized the freedom of conscience and not the freedom of expression. Codified beliefs and rituals were a way of neutralizing ideas thought to be a potential threat to state tyranny and the holy order. Cash payments renovated the Colonus-colonate bond. Feudalism, then mercantilism, elicited the psychosomatic social afflictions necessary for proliferating capitalistic views. The Voyagers went from being social phenomenon records guardians and tomb raiders to being involved in the buying, relocating, and selling of human beings. Echoes from industrial revolution graveyards stimulate fantasies.

The Calvinist's doctrine of predestination delicately insinuated that fortune is a sign of virtue. Their contentious perception of wealth progressively eroded the stigma which the influential Catholic Church had attached to extortion. Wealth accumulation is accompanied by a great deal of variation in the consolidation of power. Moneyers percolate through despicable concepts under the auspices of politicians and lumpen-intellectuals. laissez moi faire are credited for plummeting the influence of monarchs over the society, commerce and trade, and politics which set up a capitalism footing. A series of British Parliamentary exploits, the Inclosure Acts passed between 1750 and 1860, removed the prior rights of local people in rural areas and forced them out. The lands seized by these acts were then consolidated and given to politically connected farmers. France was the first country in Europe to have the ideological and rhetorical justification of the free market. In other parts of the western world, the maneuvers had different ballads with the same results of pushing the destitute men, women, and children into the firm grip of moneyers.

Global cohesion is perpetually wrapped in a blanket of apocryphal stories. For better or for worse, the proliferation of non-native concepts separates communities from their natural equilibrium. The seeds of faith in capitalism are sown deep within its mystified historical progression. The apostles of laissez-faire have repeatedly denied or dismissed the maxim contradictions in theory and praxis, and tried to nudge us out of that zone. Adam Smith's laissez-faire approach meant that there was no need for a chaperon in commerce and trade. Bernard Mandeville had faith in adequately channeled laissez-faire efforts by office-bearers. The essay of theorists such as Sir James Stuart, Johann Heinrich Gottlob Justi, François de Salignac de la Mothe-Fénelon, and Charles-Louis de Secondat points out the social setting of early modern Europe. Their overall arguments recognized the inviolability of private property as a means of creating wealth in any conceivable way.

The nearer we search into the eighteenth-century, the more we convince ourselves of their vehemence in rebuking discriminating birthrights that determine individual and group bargaining positions. On the contrary, they had the temerity to believe that fighting for a rule by the one-person principal, and everything that it entails, was a quintessentially scholarly thing to do. They nodded to brutal martinets to harmonize moneyers' rapacity and demolish the power of local guilds. They were the best and brightest pro-capitalism contingent who came up with erudite-sounding arguments to justify why moneyers were entitled to do what they wanted. Today, lasses-faire embroiders the eighteenth-century public good's optimism over the untrammeled pursuit of individual gain.

If you cannot resist the temptation of being an asshole, capitalism bills acedia as an essential noble trait for grandeur. This is more of an old social arrangement to enhance the bond among moneyers than the outcome of society's genuine sentiment of the greatest good for the greatest number. The intrinsic worth of the labor of the poor is set by captains of industries who are assisted by lumpen-intellectuals, from which all the comforts of their lives arise. The capitalistic arrangement is built on something that is no longer true. Population's linear growth, which is at the core of productivity, a capitalism prophecy, is a delusion. Old misconceptions have immeasurably widened the psychological gap between generations. Gone are the days when the army of illiterates sought secure employment and required clear and concise orders.

The polished manorialism which still exists in its pure form in a place like the Dominican Republic is fast losing legitimacy in the eyes and hearts of growing legions of the disoriented. The savvy working class is unmoved by laissez-faire banderols. The embodiment of the status quo's repudiation lies in the drift towards laissez moi faire. Collective anxiety casts doubt over the perception of an organic demarcation between individuals as well as the "have it all" nations and the "have craps". Régimes are having difficulties conducting business as public institutions by upholding nonsensical rituals and ghettoizing the masses' civic rights. Governments are hard-pressed to morph into private enterprises which entail lining equably the pocket of shareholders, its citizens. Moneyers and policymakers should be in dying need for a new compelling argument to substantiate their assertions of capitalism as the paradigm to a better society; and yet, they do not. Critical examination of the possibilities for a fresh approach has made little headway. No concrete proposal of how capitalism's sins would be overcome exist, to be examined. In the absence of a realistic alternative trajectory, we are left with no other choice than embracing enlightening disruption and letting the implosion happen on its own, so the new can emerge. Except that it is an arduous path up the hill, wicked humans cannot help themselves from attempting to tilt fate in their favor.

Most children cannot bear to see animals getting hurt. As we get older, we come to terms with traumatic nature's harmony. There is some obscure nostalgia in a stray cat cornering and tormenting a mouse for a long hour instead of butchering it. Is the cat honing its hunting skills, or an act of malicious intent? Complex questions have humbling answers. Letting nature take its course makes the predator-prey setting seem pleasant. The rule of no interference has also been an excuse for bluestockings to rest and watch messy human synchronization unfold. Even well-fed cats leave a trail of smashed corpses for their owners to deal with. It is, quite frankly, how these intemperate marauders seduce humans. In places overrun with mice and rats, having a predator around keeps down the population of pests, which in turn tampers down clashes for resources amongst their kind.

"A poor man is like a foreigner in his own country."
—ALI IBN ABI TALIB

Senseless melodies are the most captivating of all. Daydreaming ceases to be the symptom of anger and becomes the chronic absence of humanism when oppression and humiliation are applied to aspirations with equal force. Every year, offspring of the best embezzlers and the most virile poor from the third world cross the vast sea to the better world. The poorest of the bunch leave their native counties and wonderlands to land with the hope of returning one day with an eagerly-coveted cure for poverty: a load of cash. They take the Western world to represent everything good about the earth and Europe as the mother of the whole world, vastly superior to them through the courage, ambition, and mental strength of its inhabitants. It makes sense. Europe subdued civilizations and enslaved other continents for centuries.

The number of those who try to live behind persecution and precarious livelihood by embarking on a perilous journey across the ocean and cultures is insignificant compared to the mass added every year to their home countries' piles of destitute. Citizens of rich nations' hideous attitudes toward new immigrants reflects their paranoia about their prosperity's ferry, soon to be overturned by the incoming "poor." This naïve nightmare is most unreasonable in itself, and is borne out of, amongst other things, the testimonies which are given by the army of illiterate newcomers themselves about what went wrong on their lands. Immigration cannot solve the problem of poverty. Wealthy nations are incessantly purging out all poor immigrants in an attempt at salvaging the purity of the national bloodline and preventing the ascent of other cultures set to be woven into the fabric of mainstream society.

How to help developing nations help themselves? Migration regrets and cultural unease incited people to return to their nightmare's point of origin. The betterment of living standards requires a set of conditions, including specifically the ability to independently participate or engagement in the current mode and debate of commerce and trade, a legal framework promoting commerce, and a physical infrastructure allowing the circulation of goods on a large scale. Many of these conditions do not currently exist in many Third World countries, although there is plenty of labor. The few who emigrate back without handcuffs have no experience in or are armed with an irrelevant understanding of western commerce and trade trickeries. With shiny badges and the air of liberators, they land and straightaway get a prime seat amongst the oppressor gangs.

The southern hemisphere suffers from an excess of poor people and defective social net structures. Social remedies indicate that princes of economics rely on the firm conviction that poverty depends on the strength of character and the will of an individual. As undernourishment and imprisonment in a closed cell shatter warriors' bravery, so a prolonged poverty's agony and the embarrassment that comes with will morph a charismatic creature into a skunk. Moral philosophers undertake to prescribe an adequate remedy for every disease of the mind. In the twentieth-century bible on commerce and trade, denationalization and deregulation are the premises for socioeconomic comfort. Lumpen-intellectuals sanctioned rescripts in order not to doubt whether marketing the transfer of public domains to cliques is superior medicine for a nation jammed by collective anger and sorrow compared to the virtues derived from social dialogue and critical analysis of the status quo.

This is the main assumption of rational man, a person who is primarily motivated by money and simple reward, and hence whose behavior is predictable. Everything has been narrowed down to the logic of individual choice under the notions that nothing on earth is enough to be shared with everybody, and humans are, by nature, lazy. Privatization is a highly praised method of curing social ailments modestly insinuated on one side of the hemisphere. When it comes to the other side of the hemisphere, this suggestion supersedes all other remedies. Harsh aid's conditionality recklessly forces the same medicine down the shittiest countries' throats. After giving all the boasted state-run disencumbrances' features a fair trial, to no one's dismay, they are of little practical use for the poor. A lack of modern capital is a significant incubus in developing countries. One needs a lot of it to ride on the privatization wild horse.

> "By the corruption of language,
> many other corruptions begin . . ."
> —ANDRÉS DE JESÚS MARÍA Y JOSÉ BELLO LÓPEZ

A journey is not determined by devotion to a sin. The seed which was in the fruit must be placed in the earth to generate a new natural cycle of life. When a little tree is grafted to the parent tree, the fruit is that of the scion who had been inserted into the parent tree. Preconceptions' rudimentary assemblage dignifies the relative value of life. Words are to be heard not with the ears only, but also with the brain, to debunk extensively abused lexemes. The prominence of a style's fruitiness over a horse sense test suggests that new perspectives are too challenging to convey undressed. Prudence while seeking to observe and to interpret meanings in context is regarded as more severe than contemptibly timid, and the institutions responsible for the conduct of academic canvassers are warned or driven away by social and financial ostracism.

Exceptionalism is like the pillar of the gods. The false sense of preeminence makes people fall in love with the shadows of their minds. The reverberation of their vain thoughts is perceived as a précis of their destiny, though it has no substantial existence apart from their folly. The same goes for creeds brightened by prejudices which induce recklessness and coldheartedness during the investigation of social, commerce and trade, and political incidents that are contemporaneous with each other. The fantastic schemes of mass manipulation are locked in a university's safe deposit box; capitalism's popularity (or other social and political constructs' tolerance) relies on the foolish and arrogant. In parts of a world where there was no horse, uhlans were thought to be monsters: half men and half beasts. Traditions that are naturally devoid of institutionalized prejudice get a supply of it out of their western trained heroes and the bible and Quran thumper who distills absurdities into fragrant beliefs.

Commerce and trade scrimmages have centered around saving and spending as if the plea for a dialogue on wealth distribution is nonsense. I have to say that present-day wealth distribution's heart-to-heart jingles are out-of-date. The world acts as if the discourse on surplus definition and portions' boundaries has long been resolved, or that it is not time yet to revisit its premise. Social sedation is the consequence of capitalists' concerted efforts to mislabel and reclassify human rights and merits. Of capitalism's offenses, the misapprehension of profit is the grossest, while the tapering of entrepreneur connotation and definition is the subtlest. Herbert Spencer's theory, "the survival of the fittest," has the same dose of evil viciousness as Darwin's biological "natural selection." The axiom has become the slogan of the oppressors and the oppressed and established Spencer's position as a bona fide capitalism barrister.

What happened since is a phantasmagoria of delusion and injustice. Once again, the exploiters and policymakers ganged up on the laborers. Somehow, somewhere, the distinction between "profit" and "surplus" became extremely fuzzy. We have now forgotten that economics was spat out of an archaic concept of social layers that maintains that most people are just inferior creatures. Racists of the first hour have creatively wrought it. After having good test scores and being trained to memorize a bunch o' facts, thoughts, and excitements, academic gurus lose sense of reality. Nowadays, no nation seriously considers the idea of the linear distribution of wealth. Even in the face of evidence that poverty is generally transmitted to the offspring (except in those circumstances associated with wars), the free market claim of guaranteeing a fair exchange between active and passive members of an enterprise is not directly contested.

> "The wage system is not altered in the slightest by the transferal
> of private capitalism to state capitalism,
> yet the wage system is the mark of exploitation."

—ERICH KURT MÜHSAM

The story of capitalism is like the journey of one of the earth's most water-wasteful demanding plants, the tomato. Initially, the conquistador found and picked a green fruit plant. With the sun and different terrains, green turned into red. Human greed has turned bloody red! The inertia of academic's conducts, spiritual rituals, and moneyers' sadism are the crucial spices for creating a catastrophe. There is a vacillating correlation between skin pigmentation and astuteness. Albeit, there is a huge gap in the level of comfort and necessities available between two worlds, in which one assesses leadership in terms of competition and the other views it as a natural selection.

English Victorian convention has locked human creativity and humanity's destruction in the same bottle. It has facilitated humans attaining the best dreams and made humanity's worst night nightmares come true. What good is a joyride on a paved road from nowhere to nowhere? The idea that education is the top most important factor in the development of a nation or the betterment of an individual standard of living is a lie. The presumption that education is immensely essential for a country and that it dramatically changes ways of thinking is not true. Education only influenced the collective way of thinking about the robber's way of amassing wealth and glory. The truth is that education does not help. Alternatively, shall I say that education makes one a good slave unless it is a means of participation, engagement, or involvement in an enterprise.

Doesn't the whole world lie open before every man, woman, and child, just as the air is accessible to birds everywhere? Does the rain fall equally on the just and the unjust, donju and self-enslaved? The correct answer to both questions is: hell, no. Since the dawn of time, humankind has hastened to the terrestrial paradise. We go through different gates. Only a few find the one where the sweetest odors are borne towards them in the air because they inherited the right key. When the rain begins to fall, the same small group pulls out their golden umbrella, which they also inherited. Whoever does elude his or her fate within any of the current social, commerce and trade, and political constructs is not a human, but a beast.

One could not but sympathize with the acquiescent anecdotal treatise on capitalism's merits, which was a tribute to the maniacs for their obsession over amassing a fortune, and for their wickedness. The Industrial Revolution repainted with fallacies the notion of labor meriting minimal resources for survival and made the western world embrace the maxim of laissez-faire. Supporting the free market meant condemning laziness and protecting civil liberty. When moneyers reached the place to which common sense deserted the global discourses and economics, having chanced to be elected umpire between social arrangements, the poor, alive or dead, became commercial commodities.

Serendipity is a delicate harmony. Our roots haunt powerless hallucinations and powerful verdicts. Distributive justice is said to accommodate laziness. This fallacy causes free marketers today to whitewash capitalism past. How can one smile without stifling the goodness of old tears? The rich are like a fungus on the forehead; microscopic parasites living off our sweat. There is no doubt that labor is a commodity. We have come to deny knowledge is as meaningful as money and land, and limit its power to circumstantial cases. Should or could the correct social transformation come through another blood-spattered uprising of the poor and the disenfranchised? No. Financial crisis outbreaks are inevitable; poverty pandemics are optional. Applying psychological insights into economists' subplots demonstrates the inherent fluidity of values which makes shoppers malleable, and at the mercy of moneyers' greed. All of this has far-reaching implications for our understanding the true essence of the twenty-first century in general, and commerce and trade in particular.

"If you want to lose your faith, make friends with a priest."
—GEORGE IVANOVICH GURDJIEFF

How has capitalism become the most adopted form of social, commerce and trade, and political arrangement? The primary factor rests upon the belief that commerce and trade flourish only in the face of clashes and antagonism between moneyers. Valid reasoning from shadowing an axiom's stream permits deceit to fructify in ordinary folks' minds. The vagueness of the terms 'economy' and 'economics' does nothing to deter people from using them all the time, as if these terms' domain applicability are without boundaries. The ambiguity results from a misreading of the nature of the beast. Abstract concepts give space for control, puffery, trickery, and indoctrination.

Economics as social science has gathered immense power over public policy debates and the human psyche. Neoclassical scavengers pretend to scrutinize phenomenon, and the "how's" and "whys" things change over time and space. In reality, these explorations focus merely on padlocked sequences and the tail end of combers. The progress toward a proper dismemberment of economic life is being held back because of the teaching of archaic theoretical tenets. This model of investigation caricatures the truth. Economists keep refurbishing the notion that poverty is fundamentally a moral failing, and a cornucopia of luxury food and amenities is proof of divinity approval. Outsiders would likewise be aghast by the supercilious narcissism and haughtily fanaticism of the sterile scientific institutions of economics. Capitalism, the last man standing, world domination success is not solely based on power or ideology, but on the foresight of capitalists to choose the right lumpen-intellectuals at the right time and place.

Capitalism's sheepdogs' firm conviction in reconstructing identities and social nothingness using variables and fixed-point theorems poses an enormous problem for docile states, just as for rich countries. The Berlin Wall physically and ideologically divided the city for more than two decades. When the concrete barrier did collapse, the weird triumph of good over evil crushed eastern Germans' privileges and simple lives. The neoclassical apostle's unwillingness to take a high risk to achieve florescent enlightenment has made them caretakers of the bitter status quo. Any deduction of legitimacy is contingent upon the cogency of the shreds of evidence. Any induction validity depends on the saneness of assumptions. To put it simply: garbage in, garbage out. Developed economies have used their central banks to persuade private banks and other financial institutions to activate market bubbles. Far too many countries on the road to the free market have found themselves mired in corruption, mismanagement, graft, and political turmoil. The collective consciousness' distress is due to the contamination of knowledge channels from sewer overflows, especially in the third world, and academia is failing to provide protection from beautifully packaged, cerebral bullshit.

> "And so the result of several years of Everybody Shareskyism,
> other than slaughtering people, is for everybody to stand around
> and stare blankly at each other."

> —LAO SHE

The world would have been a murkier place if it was not for steadfast philosophers and militants who had a sense of right from wrong. They dared to speculate that we are animals; not only blacks, but every human species. They felt apprehensive about the environmental impact of their contemporaries' obsession with wealth and how to amass it. They were fed up with the exploitative arrangement and attempted to break capitalism's spell. Their efforts were in vain. During colonization, aboriginals' sweat and hard work became profit, but the privileges it entails is applied to only Caucasians. Our collective wisdom has yet to find a crack in what is perceived as an insurmountable immoral wall. Scores of countries with low-grade, common-sense dysplasia have taken it upon themselves to try to substitute the neoliberal paradigm of market solutions with other forms of socially biased truths and false prophecies. There is a glut of social speculation on damaged logic. Several antidotes to injustice are based on the belief that poverty depends on the character and the will of an individual. At every junction in which the dominant feature is widespread coercion, this principle is unquestionably true for robbers, rapists, and impostors. For other ways of livelihood, this is blasphemy.

The mainstream conception of human behavior, the economic man, does not take into account instinct or habit formation. Mutineers' skepticism leads them to question the deliberate misinterpretation of the social agents' reactions and capitalism's supremacy. A choice between a prospect or gamble scenario obviates the nature of being human and highlights economists' hallucinations. In a society in which Machiavellian methods for getting rich or tightening social order is regarded as assisting in the betterment of the only surviving species of the genus homo (or a contribution to the union), any real social justice experiment is doomed. Economics is a serial liar and fantasist's domain. As long as patriotism supersedes reflection and ideology rules instead of critical thinking, glory and misfortune is called wealth and poverty; it is the symbol of pointless debate. It doesn't come as a surprise to anyone that capitalism is a dysfunctional system, except that it has a psychological contract that no one wants to break.

By the end of the twentieth century, every social, commerce and trade, and political construct underwent more than a rhinoplasty in a desperate effort to escape responsibility. A global system underlying the extremely unequal distribution of wealth and power has kept the profane views of the labor class and hierarchical arrangements between commerce and trade actors the same. Conspiracy rules and success myths do work. Every existing doctrine compresses the ambiance of the love affair with untamable disillusions. Thanks to capitalism, as the story goes, poor white women and children were recognized as humans. Somehow, everyone else also found their way through the golden age of self-enslavement and into the human centipede as efficient slaves. "Le Roi est mort, vive le Roi!"

8

Echography of the Twenty-First Century

"Human development is a form of chronological unfairness,
since late-comers are able to profit by the labors of their predecessors
without paying the same price."

—ALEKSANDR IVANOVICH HERZEN

MULTIFARIOUS CHANGES OCCURRED AT the end of the twentieth century. Things didn't go quite well, as the cycle requires. As we reached the threshold, our courage wavered. Instead of subduing our anxiety, it asphyxiated us. Moneyers have since defecated on the collectivist spirit until pictures of the depressions and world wars inundated the world. Habit-forming inventions seduced us and synchronized theism, art, and science's abrasive and arrogant approach. Mercenaries and bilkers came to inspire an entire generation, for a moment. Vassals or herds of moneyers' avaricious motivations made a number of cities in West hubs of creativity, and went on to influence most of the world. The yoked nations' social, commerce and trade, and political leashes loosened. We learned a lot about humans. For third world activists who wanted to be heard, there were specific, designated sides of the hemisphere where they had an incomparable chance to do so. By Sigmund Freud's well-regarded exposé, at some point, every Western boy will neurotically crave a piece of his mother's tail. Lunatics abused ninetieth-century philosophers' contentions to attack conventions.

We disremembered that globalization didn't orchestrate the remarkable multicultural migration; aircraft turbine engines did.

The twentieth century is marked by the adroitness of humanity's social and political acumen thwarters, economists. Economics had its hand in everything. Despite the free marketers' reputation for mistaking noises for signals, the entire world put them on a pedestal. Lumpen-intellectuals fooled us with a constellation of ornaments. They dragged the social justice discourse further down a recklessness path. Their disgraceful exploits abetted moneyers, setting the world on the road to self-annihilation. Alternatives to the free market progressively lost ground due to their preachers' lack of extrasensory perception. Communists sins and socialism's never-ending commerce and trade slump has spawned a general pessimism and predisposes a country to embrace neo-liberalism. Other factions prematurely optimized their perceptions of the now.

It is in the mist of the servitude's refinement that the newest global social paradigm was molded. Désolé, Karl Marx's butterfly shenanigan of capitalism to socialism's cycle, was implausible. Even in a purely capitalistic setting, people can't buy or sell their labor like they buy and sell goods and services. Marx's conceptual flaws are unabashed romanticism, imbedded in his theory of alternatives to capitalism. In his reading of the next social paradigm drift, he failed to realize that capitalism doesn't create class conflict; rather, its innate protocols establish socially adaptable and diffusible tensions. But Marx's spiritual authority has not lost its influence upon flamboyant counter-capitalism drives.

The accruing means of reaching further back into history safeguards rituals and resentment and inspires grisly aspirations. Bold ideas and bold solutions always sprung out to help humanity fight its way through freedom from idiocy. Schools were founded to focus on producing an educated elite class, not engineering elites nor bloating the faction that controls a disproportionate amount of wealth, privilege, or political power in society. With the mid-twentieth century global expansion of education, the laboring class's noble motivation metamorphosed the poor into a class of working poor, the self-enslaved. The true essence of post-World War II is mass access to an institution of knowledge and learning. This is the most underappreciated direct consequence of the twentieth century robber barons and captains of industrial, social, commerce and trade, and political sentiment shifts.

Penitence!!!

"Who lives sees, but who travels sees more."

—IBN BATTUTA

What is it really like to be human in the twenty-first century? Few people are making unimaginable fortunes, while most are still scraping a living out of the dry ground. Devices insert global points of view into insulated societies' ongoing deliberations. The most grotesque wish on my bucket list is to travel with the heart of a vacationer, a schmuck, instead of being a human visiting crappy countries. The numerous clusters of bulbous nerve endings upon the tongue by no means has ubiquitous control over the composite sense of taste. The journey into unusual emotional intelligences is bottomless. Gallivanting around the world with humanist beliefs fades the vastness of space and ethos between isolated spots. Social issues initially deemed as exceptional incidents are revealed to be large scale, virulent, and overwhelmingly complex; except that being a wanton critic of everything leads to the taste of mortals' wobbly conjoint peculiarities. We subscribe or are complicit in monstrosities, and to bugaboos of beautification.

Economics has developed an appearance of sapience. Slavish trust comes in many flavors. Facts learned from perusing manuscripts or hot tips uncovered from the deep web make a colloquy fascinating, but it isn't the same as knowing something. In order to draw a distinction between a hum and a howl, one has to walk outside and withstand humanity's inconsistencies and idiosyncrasic surges. The certain paradigm shifts inherent to humankind's perpetual renovations keep relevant the context in which phenomena occur. Developing knowledge from direct experiences outside of a conventional setting backdropped with golden sprays rips up the rules and harmonies of the twenty-first century's examination.

Mythical wealth's accumulation steps have a grip on the poor anima. Conformists believe in capitalism and folktales, and have faith in its ostensible coherence. Normal folks embark on messianic crusades as they believe that the most effective way of attaining social, commerce and trade, and political utopia are through capitalistic conventions. Society's focal point is oriented towards ideologues that can round up followers. They yank people into believing in beliefs rather than believing in a belief. Lumpen-intellectuals massively play a fundamental role in inspiring, guiding, and directing the public's lopsided sentiments on social, commerce and trade, and political issues; whereas religious institution guidelines for what is right and wrong debilitate hominids longing for emotional autonomy. Lucrative ambitions and narcissism underline the circumstantial parallel between lumpen-intellectuals and religious public manipulation styles. Poor folks surrender their rights to the two and feel a contractual obligation to fulfill their duties of upholding outrageous principles by any means necessary.

Science and art have infused the world with an overwhelming sense of redemption. Creativity is the quintessence of the present-day priority which is pushing boundaries of the unknown, on the double. New technological applications are treated as pathways to society's bright future. Restricted cultures are tossing out elements of archaic social constructs and are also living off of these redecorations. Gadgets have engendered the supreme intrusion on our primitive instincts, and mock individualism. The psychological devaluation of traditional financial institutions' powers over money transfer value has triggered a reassessment of the deep-seated notion of currency. Cryptocurrency vows to abrogate bank and government jurisdictions over money. Digital currency with no intrinsic weight is amending the existing perception of money. Meanwhile, gunning down suppressed big cats is the asshole's contribution to their former colony's tourism industry.

Social examiners used a razor blade to cut away humanity's epidermis to reveal what's going on underneath. Setting up a Bellagio's classically bonded, leather-tufted chaise (with Ottoman-Bellagio buttons) in the center of a town will get people gabbing away secrets. For penny-pinching sleuths, there is a less cunning, but it's a parsimonious tactic to urge people to talk about every detail of their lives; to be human. Despite our cultural contrasts, human beings act and react similarly in impassioned transactional situations. Currently, we are all maneuvering to fall into the middle class. The most comforting feeling in the middle of the sinking Titanic was certainly not being in the rear deck, the first pile of people to disappear into the ocean. The sight of the ship's captain, crew, and the rich twirling on the front deck was perhaps inspirational. Desires underpinning human behavior are really old. The essence of our quest fundamentally remains the same. Outwardly, the permanence and universality of the most evident social and political folly is paradoxical to humanity's overall ambitions and shared talents.

> "Everyone designs who devises courses of action aimed
> at changing existing situations into preferred ones."
>
> —HERBERT ALEXANDER SIMON

A ray of light shining brighter in the dark is not always a good sign. We embellish the twenty-first century's conflicting two-story painting. The flamboyance of the canvas colors depicts the privilege and arrogance of the ones who work hard to keep the dice rolling up right for them. The background is crammed with the emasculated bodies of the naïve working poor doing all the hard work. The beauty of this chef-d'oeuvre would mislead even a connoisseur to contest distinct biological prejudice, and points out class struggle. In every nook and cranny of the world, the rich always appear to impart profound and prodigious capacities far exceeding the poor. During the medieval era, slave servants saw children from rich families being schooled by a private tutor at home, and watched them grow up to become their children's masters. People with knowledge have always been highly honored by their countrymen. Hence, to the eyes of the poor, knowledge means a safe, secure net worth.

To deny colonization mindset is still shaping the third world's current state of affairs is either stomach-churning naivety or cruel insolence. The masters left to their former colonies the culture of shitty governance, massive mineral wealth misused and pocketed by the few to the detriment of many, and education system that leads to no jobs. The trauma of cold war chronicles is being given a second life, with the wealthy nations scrambling to secure a natural resources saga. Western financial scavengers, memories raiders, and bullish adolescents, with the help of international organizations' muscles and long arms, are playing a role in constricting third world conversations around the ascendancy of democracy. Their triumph is not on fecund vices such as corruption or corruptibility. They wouldn't be able to realize their monstrous fantasies without the gyrations of post-colonization's submissive generations of complicity (or, at least, complacency). For the apparent sickening reason of the asinine premise, a tyrant's firm grip is necessary in order for a nation to succeed and take its future into their own hands, and is said to be applied only to the southern hemisphere. Flawed notions romanticize the struggle for social justice anywhere in the world.

A human is not, by nature, a docile creature. Subservience can germinate under favorable conditions or by severe and prolonged spirit mutilation. Regardless of time period or culture, truculent enslaved men and women were always consigned to lifelong torture or other cruel, inhuman treatments or punishment. Shackles were not only used to restrict movement, but to humiliate defiant individuals. Slavery ceased to be the conventional mode of production. The slaves have since melted into the vast throng of the destitute. The ignominy of being enslaved is far worse than being dirt poor. But any prolonged ill treatment ebbs away self-esteem. People lose the sense of their rights, and what is right.

The weight of oppression lingers longer in the emotional fragments that carry the instructions of thought process. It is a powerful contributor to some undying glitches in the poor's problem assessment and decision-making methods. Free marketers' unrelenting propaganda, political actions, and the rich display of their lavish lifestyles has emboldened the poor to push all of their chips into prospects that hew to capitalism's hypocritical motto. One thing could be said about men and women who embrace their horrible fate: they conspire assiduously for their offspring's emancipation. Their harsh living conditions is a potent impetus to envisage and plot for their kids a lavish lifestyle with a horde of servants and a pool full of bullion coins. There is no written statement: the labor class perceived that education is a way of accumulating wealth and increasing the share of power. Society's stratification still has the moneyers on the top and labor at the bottom. Poor people who rip their hearts out get tied up with golden shackles, and they amount to nothing more than despicable assholes.

"They blame the people when the blame is on the system."
—FILIBERTO OJEDA RÍOS

The balloon filled with the poor is not decreasing, as it potentially could. Economists unequivocally claim that proletarians only need a multidimensional training and quality job search to get pecuniary returns on their improved brains. The key to a first-class existence deliberately omits the social and political context. Nothing could be farther from the truth. The notion of education as a remedy for all humankind's problems, especially poverty, has been proven to be an argument of ignorance regardless of an adopted commerce and trade dogma. Education alone doesn't break poverty's constraints.

The ones at the bottom of the social pyramid are oftentimes accused of being reluctant to undertake cerebral drills. Such derogatory remarks disregard proletarian struggles of having to stay longer on the rat wheel in order to make enough to sustain their existence. The worthless quality of higher education in crappy nations is worsening the global standing of their poor. Rain does fall equally on the just and the unjust; however, we don't all have an umbrella; nor are we all bold. The rate of technological change now is greater than in the recent past. It has become a pretext for ignoring the army of the unemployed despair.

A parallel can be drawn between the deliberate killing of the Moriori by the Maori over karaka berries in the midst of the Pacific Ocean, and the Mayans by conquistadors searching for gold on the new continent. Customers' lures were refined with Aristide Boucicaut selling goods at fixed prices and tolerating exchanges and refunds. Better than in The Grands Magasins Dufayel, Harry Gordon Selfridge made common folk feel like royalty. Gerold Lauck and Edward Bernays convinced us that consumerism is the best instrument for self-emancipation because materials are the only expression of true love. Commerce and trade have since taken a better view, but our collective conscience is limping. The charming cliché's anthem, globalization or one world, is diverting humanity's attention from the continuous repulsiveness of the world's state of affairs. The cliché has degraded the quality of wants. Globalization has intensified overconsumption and sprung out of the latest customers' breed: shoppers who have a shameless sense of entitlement.

In every glamorous city, one doesn't need to dive into its underbelly to cross-examine and photograph people in the most desperate of circumstances. The shinning parts of the world are currently experiencing a partial loss of memories and apathy caused by the drawn-out pause between their regional blood-shedding cyclic peaks. We don't need to scratch deeper into human memory to dilute the westernized and aesthetic façade of the southern hemisphere.

The free market has been crowned as the summit of social, commerce and trade, and political models; beyond which there is nowhere left to climb. The concept has reduced the world to an asylum run completely by the inmates and the working poor. Indolence is prolonged while fewer and fewer people can honorably achieve the ideal of well-being. Commerce and trade maestros whisper foolishness in economics purpose and nature only to each other; then turn around and propagate rules underlaid by concepts a hundred years out of date. Making capitalistic social arrangements better is a transcending obsession. The crux of commerce and trade debate is deliberately esoteric. The trained observe the samurai code of loyalists. Exclusiveness extends trivialities in the overly narrow research on economics.

Evidence of pervasive social injustices in a particular area of surplus creation and distribution doesn't produce howls of outrage from the public. For the one-percenters and the little bourgeois assertions that global socioeconomic injustices claims are nothing more than a fallacious attack on capitalism. The public is less vulnerable or voiceless than ever before. The democratization of knowledge and the wider circle of public participation are felt in the partisan nature of politics. The freer people get, the more confident they get. Freedom and confidence don't automatically activate common sense neurons. Sharp people who second-guess their doctors wouldn't dare challenge economics dogma. Doyens wrestle with present-day complex social, commerce and trade, and political disputes using prejudiced reinterpretations of old manuscripts. The global restless angst-ridden mood is ignored as if an apocalypse could never happen. Most people are already offended before ever encountering the substance of the counteroffer to capitalism.

> "The old man died beneath the wheels of the twentieth century.
> There was nothing left but stains, bloodstains, and fragments of
> flesh . . . And the same thing is happening to my generation."
> —DAMBUDZO MARECHERA

In the west, commerce and trade view wrangling is taking precedence over political melodramatic scuffles. The expectations about leadership are changing because social agents and patterns have to derail old concepts of nation-state and power. The standard of living improvement has fostered social capacity innovations and has altered community bonds between leaders and followers. Time and time again, national distrust flares up and raises higher the levels of citizen commitment to irrational anthems and creeds. In some countries, social absurdity is continuously entrenched in their dialogues.

Avid bandits are relocating entire national wealth and natural resources control of the third world to the first world. It is naïve to underscore this pattern of collective neglect by modern economies, and is a distinct threat to global security. As a result of profit repatriation by foreign companies to their countries of origin, they plant a décor for rich to poor and create a win-lose agenda leading to heartrending results upon the host land. Their action intensifies the bleak outlook of the disenchanted left in the mire. There is a limited number of ways to dance this mambo correctly. The legitimate scope of contemporary form of cash expansion should require each nation on the negotiation table to respect the claims of justice for all. There is more to the real story.

It is not easy to make a decision when every alternative requires a high dose of evil. The developing nations today face a role model dilemma in selecting the most elegant way of pulling themselves out of the socio-economic sewer. The coveted countries' blueprints are all sketched with a bloody ink pen. The plot with the highest probability of success holds devastating costs in term of collective wisdom.

The perception of chic enslavement in reality rationalizes ruining the social fabric, except that they want to neutralize pervasive poverty by jumping into twenty-first century commerce and trade while holding on tightly to their primeval hunter-gatherer arrangements, beliefs, and rituals. Another option lies in following in the footsteps of highly developed nations by developing an impressive defense industry, then emboldening the oppressed to rebel against tyrants, which generates new orders from totalitarian regimes for weapons to crush any resistance, and military technology to spy on the masses. There is also the subliminal conquest of a nations rich in natural resources and the externalization of the social and political mess, which is the most proven high-yield scheme of all.

Long after independence, preposterous terms of privileges and rights continue to trigger collisions and massacres. Antediluvian mores are firm bastions of factions' self-admiration. Group demarcations based on physiognomy and petty habits have pervaded mundane routine and conventions. The emaciation of poor nations is primarily due to endogenous factors such as an inhabitant's defective benchmark of leadership traits. The colonial-contrived social brackets continue to place dialogues along the fault lines of identity. As control continues to build, the remnants of colonization's tradition continues to arbitrate socioeconomic disputes.

An often overlooked, yet critically important, factor is the extent to which urbanization in third world countries is propelling egoism. A case could be easily made that the nature of poor countries' individualism is worse than in their rich counterparts. Conformism is noticeable on the part of their intelligentsia. It doesn't stem from the moral pressures and the reprisals to which dissenters have often been subjected. Pernicious individualism is trapping every third world class's layers in devastating wars and prodigalities far beyond corruption and corruptibility. Current western public inclusive hypocrisy and the rest of the world which is acculturated to it circumvents such testimony as patronizing undeveloped nations.

Old societies sought the help of the supernatural to spot the new-born with the evilest genes who would lead epic predation. A leader's viciousness was universally the source of domestic pride. History commemorates groups tainted by insatiable appetites who subjugate their weak neighbors and expand their territory. Self-denigration produces sufficient misperception to lower common-sense levels. The modern emaciation of a poor nation can be attributed to endogenous factors, such as its defective benchmark of leadership traits. In a society in which narcissism is the most esteemed human attribute, the air is full of obsequious bows and the leitmotifs of the debates lack any other ingredient than politics. When it comes down to choosing a leader, it's all about the hobgoblin with the highest ability to trick the mass of intellectual homunculus, or the vitality to resist mental and physical onslaught. People would simply refuse to admit their chosen ones' sins and would recklessly support them to the grave. Fidelity tied to religion, ethnicity, and class supersedes national interest. This ridiculous bonding feeds leaders' megalomania.

The developing countries' misperception of man as a political animal has become vital to the rest of world's wobbly opulence and expansion and the next global financial crisis's postponement. In the shittiest part of the globe, the delusion of grandeur and the daft egoism of the elite are of the same tenacity as the disgraceful individualism of the masses. The do-gooders are concerned with making and implementing injustices according to fair processes. The southern hemisphere shitholes accept even outcomes they do not like, or more suffering, when the procedures that are adopted from high-rises in the West respect their stupid mores and rites. This part of the world is a long way from alleviating the neo-colonial syndrome and moving the core of their discussion beyond politics. The trails of blood of their heroes are left behind as they were severely beaten and dragged into boilers by drunk monkeys starting and ending in the south.

> "The commodity originally appears upon
> becoming the property of some person."
>
> —KOZO UNO

The perpetual flow of historic tweaks constantly alters individual as well as groups' roles within society. As far as commerce and trade, over time, humanity's social swings and political brawls has morphed once-simple commodity exchange and simple commodity production into Machiavellian maneuvers and voracious curiosity interplays. Commerce and trade participants' distinct behaviors are inherent to the nature of the bazaar, and to time. Please keep in mind that the saga was, is, and will always be between merchants and customers.

In the old days, the Radanites roamed through vast territories, urging royalty and common folk to buy their goods. Merchants' impotent possibilities and frontiers restricted the options offered to customers, while religious sermons dried out peasants' joie de vivre. These two constraints made souks' assortments deficient in their vibrancy. The classical conditioning of Pavlov scripts the interplay between sellers and buyers. In a primitive market in which commodities are predictable, the notion of utility has merit.

Moving away from mercantilism, wealth's modus operandi changed from piling up bullions to the assiduous dehumanization of certain groups of people in an avalanche of slavery. Human bondage is an efficient tool when the freely accessible source of nutrients is deliberately made inadequate. These social factors morphed merchants into producers and customers into consumers. There were constant clashes between the producers' motives and the consumers' values. Captains of industries used the principle of *vis et voluntas* to rule over labor and consumers.

Philosophers such as Bernard de Mandeville saw a dose of vice in the "Christian virtues" of his time as indispensable for the blossoming and booming of commerce and trade. The ascendance of capitalism in its ripe form (mutilated on every side) included merchants and customers, the onus of commerce and trade. Spirituality failed to confine merchants and customers' euphoria and required a set of conditions, including specific technological innovations of mass production and a legal framework promoting egoism. Mid-twentieth century social and political shifts put to rest the merchants' meekness and customers' boring roles, once and for all. Merchants' motives for making a ton of mazuma without sweating have earned them the 'moneyer' badge; whereas customers have become shoppers, their values driven by a desire to experience pleasure or fulfillment without delay or deferment. In this era, politicians pushed for big infrastructure projects allowing the circulation of goods on a large scale, and openly aided moneyers' private accumulation.

The sentiment of society during Plato's time was that "money-makers are tiresome company, as they have no standard but cash value," moneyers' gains by or benefits from others through compliancy or complacency. In the capitalistic jurisdiction, merchants are ruthless moneyers, and their motive is to make a ton of money. This ignoble objective requires figuring out how to break customers' indifference. Common Era enterprises, with the help of a clicktivist's battalion, are all centered around conjuring up customer deliriums. Merchants more enthusiastically imagine and spit out new stuff with complementary functionality, than produce monotonous essentials. Nowadays, merchants endlessly ruminate on befitting wily procedures to make their traps work. Enterprise's preference for a customer's indifference seems limitless when blended with romantic stimuli, intellectual intimidations, and an individualized consideration for common folk. The full power of preference has been passed on from sellers to producers rather than to moneyers. In the twenty-first century, moneyers can't compel or coerce customers, but rather, influence shoppers to take action or perform an activity.

> "Today we are experiencing the notion
> of influencer and influenced."
>
> —JOSÉ JULIÁN MARTÍ PÉREZ

No one is beautiful. What we are is a convex projection of oneself. Curved or bulged inwards, our persona appears thin and tall to others. Who we are is a concave projection of oneself. Curved or bulged outwards, our self-esteem appears short and fat to ourselves. We now have at our disposal an unimaginable quantity of trappings to exaggerate the features of our caricature. The inflated complexity of this hoodwinked perception creates a parallel potential for a delusional sense of being beautiful. It is a psychological quagmire.

In the twenty-first century, humans collectively spend more time sculpting, promoting, and retuning foods and stuff than on farming or producing amenities. The moneyer's thirst and shoppers' ache are the freshest essences of the commerce and trade waltz. Our examination of commerce and trade has not made any significant progress. Economists abuse the term 'scarcity' in order to thwart moneyers' influences and shoppers' impulses, and to draw nifty graphs. This cunning approach has had far-reaching repercussions. The dismemberment of commerce and trade interplays is starting to be infused with socially inclusive approaches. Newfangled rationalizations of moneyers' influences and shoppers' impulses are steadily brewing. Customers are absolutely unmoved by merchants' concerted efforts to purvey ecstasy unless a basket of specific values assigned to an item validates their impulse. To put it in the most simplification form: a customer's indifference depends on exchange settings, intuitive feelings, and the fact of continuing to exist. The implications of these propositions are key to the chapter on Tabula Rasa in this book. There is more to this than meets the collectivist's eye.

We have long agreed that human nature isn't fixed. Human nature is central to widening the confusion concerning why we do what we do. At first glance, human routines appear quite absurd. Science's binoculars heave social causes such as poverty, inequality, and unemployment forward. The superficial intellectualization of human nature makes context and insight equally critical to understanding any creature's propensity of actions. Social reflections frame customers' pursuit of fulfillment on a caprice contingency scale. Technological innovations shed new light on the complexity of cells' control systems and reveal that what humans for so long thought were inner voices or a soul are, rather, biological receptors. Biologists have ceased to adhere to the antiquated works of Hippocrates and Galen. Given the radical advancement of science and technology in the last few decades, it is an offense to dissect commerce and trade actors on the receiving end, disregarding major breakthroughs in neuroscience. Humans' actions and reactions boil down to neurotransmitters which play a major role in shaping everyday life and functions. A neurotransmitter subliminally influences customer actions through a remarkable number of mechanisms.

> The five traditional senses are physiological capacities of organisms. They play a role in converting some external physical signals to neural signals that the brain can understand. In Greek mythology, Zeus handed Pandora a box and said she was not to open it, but she opened it anyway, and released all diseases and evils into the world. Temptation is welded to proximity in space. Propinquity is key to attraction. Proximity's value was the customers' dominant factor, which marks the pre-mercantilism era.

> The human gut is an enteric nervous system sustenance value or, as neuroscience experts call it, our second brain. This value stamped the capitalistic social progress paradox as communal lands were taken away from peasants, and the notion of trading one's time for a means of subsidence became prevalent. The consequence of the unskilled laborer's increased density in cities lead to the pervasiveness of universal subordination to physiological necessaries and sustenance's value.

> The ability to respond to stimuli is a fundamental characteristic of living organisms. The central nervous system collects information about changes in its environment, both internal and external. It processes information and often relates it to previous experiences.

One remarkable feature is the speed of the response, which is virtually instantaneous. Sentimental value is a purely psychological necessity manufactured by positive occurrences or phantasms. It is a symptom of the twenty-first century's new paradigm.

On paper, the customer's propensity for action can decidedly be anticipated by means of observation or experience as well as theory. Self-motivation to acquire an item or to subscribe to a service is, in essence, an instant mental assessment of values attached to its tag price. It is the same as saying that customer indifference towards it is more than zero. The cyclical change of a particular customer's value greatly depends on the set of social and political conditions. Our sensory mechanism has played a great role in our primitive emotions. Marketing schemes' vitality in the Anno Domini era is an evidence of customer indifference and fluidity.

Data assembling and human interaction's revolution brought a sea of changes into play. It has altered the nature of money and land, and prepped labor. The industrial revolution's leading man was assailed with waves that shrunk his main d'oeuvre muscles. Body mass is no longer the pool barrier to factory efficiency. The Von Neumann–Morgenstern axioms are now exclusively factoring in merchant decision-making processes and do not apply anymore to customers psyches. Enterprises have become sophisticated at mapping customers' impulses patterns. Fashion's lifespan is constantly shrunken. Financial institutions dilute the distance between our fingers and our bank accounts. Item swaps are mediated virtually. Enterprises count on expertise or ingenuity to reach deep into customer minds and wallets. Moneyers' wickedness and shoppers' limitless cravings are threats to every form of life. There is no way to put a break on the trend caused by the expansion of scientific knowledge's applications. Applying psychological insights into economists' subplots demonstrates the inherent fluidity of values and makes shoppers malleable and at the mercy of moneyers' greed. All of this has far-reaching implications for understanding the bizarre beings we have become in general, and for commerce and trade in particular.

"Looking Backward was written in the belief that
the Golden Age lies before us and not behind us."

—EDWARD BELLAMY

The twentieth century was one of bloodshed and violence under the false pretense of socio-political dogmas. Operation Condor, the crusade of radical repression and horror in Latin America, had nothing to do with capitalism versus evil communism. Beneath the surface and behind the façade, twenty-first century enthusiasm is not enough to cure the malaise permeating the entire world. We have long agreed that we ought to conceptualize a social transformation podium and embark on the easier task of grasping the new paradigm we do live in. The counterpunch to capitalism has turned out to be pure chindogu. The rash design and assembly of items, concepts, and obsessions is an indication of humanity converging towards one single point: the death of creativity.

I wish that long gone was the time when intellectualism was a sin of the elite, and common folks regarded any study of physics and astronomy as the highest calling. We are still in a deep cerebral semi-vegetated state, at least ninety-nine percent of the time. I feel bilious every time I assess squadrons who are taken by banal social movements and hullabaloo over political parties. How best to depict the twenty-first century's global socioeconomic nebulous trajectory? A few arrogant, selfish, and judgmental creatures are pushing global welfare to the brink of collapse, aggressively taunting Mother Nature. Theorists are liquidating queer reasoners, and the rest of the world is cheering for them. While social derailment is happening, traditional blocs fund choirs of eunuch's scholars to charm and to hypnotize us with subliminal tunes and the aroma of cerebral defecation. Most observations on "intermerce" are mostly inaccurate, not surprising conclusions; and prescribed remedies are often dead wrong.

What good is a joyride on a paved road from nowhere to nowhere? The idea that education is the top most important factor in the development of a nation or the betterment of an individual standard of living is a lie. Learning at the college or university level only influenced the collective way of thinking about the robbers' way of amassing wealth and glory. The truth is that education does not help. Alternatively, shall I say, education makes one a good slave unless it is a means of participation, engagement, or involvement in an enterprise's preferred method of trying to break shoppers' indifference.

Many, if not most, scholars feel like the duty imposed upon them is to dazzle their fellow human beings, and genuflecting to crooks in order to advance their careers. The meek join factions sanctioned as doctrines. They morph into the best primitive form of themselves to move up the ranks. The plucky have the natural inclination to build a consensus around irrational belief by filling up the empirical gap to make a case for injustice. The way to safeguard their inadequacies is by dipping in and out of reality and then caricaturing it. They are known as total evil creatures and want to impose their distributive justice ideal differently, ranging from rigging the system to mass slaughter. Demi-gods impose an internally consistent approach for artistic and scientific inquiry by replicating the uniformity of nature in the physical universe without the meaning and effect of the character in social life's non-uniformity. Explaining concepts by employing a purely axiomatic process leaves no place for reflection. The asymmetry of theories and reality extend further into prejudiced consumption.

The entire world is hectically filling up knowledge potholes to fulfill the caprice of the one side of earth that we all have come to rely on and envy. Wealthy peoples' recklessness is exhausting humanity's growth. The story of quiet, shitty nations is that their testimony to peace is not the socioeconomic improvement trigger, nor a green light. Peace itself is relative. Poor nations' legislatures are directly beholden to the whims of eccentric western tycoons. Their citizens' ineptitude towards participation, engagement, or involvement in contemporary discourse or commerce and trade, and their choppy and amateurish ambitions, are overlooked. The eastern and southern hemisphere's standards have not changed the geometry of human wants and needs. Antiquated traditions which incorporated the old tenants' airs, vainglory, and religion are all part of the third world's infecund ecosystem. The west political engineering realities have left the east, north, and south facing a monstrous dilemma. In their attempts to prevent the noxious frustration, resentment, and blind hatred from slipping gently into their irrigation systems, they justify horrific homicide.

Immense fortunes are created by betting on humanity's triumphs and catastrophes. Math wizards are stamping a price tag on any and everything, a trade in which common sense is epileptic. People gauge hourly how much and how far from the top and the bottom they are, to phony up some joie de vivre. We press on, categorizing quick interactions and assigning sensations to appearance. The embraced culture's obsolescence doesn't preclude originality. Wasteful and insatiable beings, superimposed in debt-ridden nations, just want originality, that doesn't last. The predominance of delusion of intellectual adequacy is a result of the higher learning sequences' ignoble commitment to social control and instant social change. The intelligentsia doesn't rule the world. Scholars are the servants, not the masters. Specific questions draw blunt answers. Who do they serve? We all, without doubt, have to own some of this mess. Public submissiveness and the moneyers' obstinacy have reached ridiculous proportions.

The ability to self-determine and to crucify any other assault that denigrates a human being as a possession is not a novelty of the twenty-first century. Moneyers and politicians have been molesting people without a stop, over and over again. Repeated global financial busts have jangled nerves and exposed deep cultural rifts. Towns which forbid the feeding of animals have measures aimed at restricting people from feeding the homeless. Self-absorption and devilry are epicene. Providing for the wealthy has reached a new high of madness. The elite no longer flocks in pint-size enclaves: reserves are being carved out of cities for them everywhere. We actively take part in or bear witness to humans bedeviling and dehumanizing their own kind. The world is fixated on substitutes for right and wrong reasoning and remains oblivious to the hidden cost of capitalism. We potentially have enough to pass around. The scarcity hypothesis sneaks wealth distribution out of the room while obscuring creativity.

The old labor theory of value suggests that relative prices of goods mirror the average number of labor hours necessary to produce it. In the twenty-first century, the quantity of labor hours is not the primary driver of prices. The speed in which human competence subjugates imaginations to ruthlessly fill up the time and space between birth and death and to aerate egos is staggering. This fast tempo has made the colonization our needs and our wants pleasantly complex for inventors and lucrative for moneyers. In doing so, instead of the average number of labor hours, the quality of the means necessary in an enterprise to produce a commodity or provide a service establishes relative prices. And an enterprise ability to break shoppers' indifference in distinction to estimate the economic value of a commodity or service fixes its profitability.

Capitalism was an organic beginning of hazardous social transformations instigated by the English industrial revolution. We feel all disconnected, more than ever before, under the still-prevailing social and political arrangement. In order to bring the moneyers' lurid "deux poids, deux mesures" plot to life, lumpen-intellectuals are mutilating the appreciation of being human. They are succeeding at branding the new cultural deviation as another phase of the industrial revolution. Apprentice experiments of multiplying poverty and crime and then subtracting reality opens the door to advanced research into economics and theology. Hardnosed scientists are mastering the art of vagueness to well serve the maniacs in getting the public to look away from the obvious solutions to their conundrum. Compassion has become a nightmare and a travesty for new age voyeur of other mortals' suffering or the indigenous upper class's illusion of everlasting opulence. We are all stitching our mouths on the asses of those more privileged than us. The world has gotten very comfortable with all dreadful forms of socioeconomic inequalities. The laboring class has morphed into being outrageous human centipedes.

The diagnostic of the twenty-first century main upheavals, wealth inequality and climate change, and the social classes' skirmishes resulting from the paradigm shift reveal that we are in dire need of a *morales nuvem consensus*. This will bring forth social, commerce, *intermerce* and political covenants appropriate to the twenty-first century and beyond.

Interview

Q: Can you tell us a bit about your background in Economics?

A: I grew up in a third world country where only two socioeconomic classes exist, the few almighty powerful on the top while the rest of the depraved masses scrambling at the bottom; and when you take the same picture and retrace the same reality through the geopolitical Cold War's implications for the national economy, everybody was a victim. That experience will make you either resigned to be a slave to the system, or you make socio-economic injustice a lifetime mission. I chose the latter, and I ended up spending enough time in stringent economic monasteries where this field is taught as a science. In time, I have come to reject that notion, and I deliberately chose the classical economists' dialectic, an approach of economics discipline as an art of social substance. Economics is an addition to my arsenal of business academic training (accounting, management and finance), philosophy, politics, and real-life tragedies. All of these elements come through in my writing content and style, which receives either scathing insults or abundant praise for not being transmitted in the "normal" economics cadence.

Q: You rage against social injustice and economic inequality; what inspired this?

A: My anger is born out of these wizards who toy around with economic models that are filled with assumptions that crap on humanity. The problem is that economics academia has been acting as if the primary inquiry, wealth distribution, has been solved. As a consequence, the field has evolved into a mechanical formulaic process of shooting out outcomes.

However, when you travel around and meet real people and witness the ravaging consequences of capitalism, you cannot help but be angry, like I am, and will want to reexamine the status quo.

Q: Your new book "Cast Away: For These Reasons: Economic Jihad" strikes at the heart of Capitalism. What's wrong with capitalism (tongue in cheek)?

A: There's nothing wrong with capitalism. It is a system which is well suited to a different world and time, when slavery was viewed as an efficient production model and bigotry was one of the respected methodologies for developing social constructs. We have come to forget that capitalism sprung up in England at a time when peasants lost their lands and didn't have any skills, and most of what was brought to the marketplaces were produced by hand. In this picture, the masses were at the mercy of the bourgeois, who possessed the ability and right to initiate an enterprise, and controlled primary means of production. This doesn't justify the social injustices inherent to capitalism, but it demonstrates how easy it was for a few culprits to enslave the laboring masses who are doled out a meager recompense, also known as a wage. The class bargaining argument has changed. In light of that shift, we can no longer stand complacent to this savage and frankly archaic economic system.

Q: Why are you in favor of casting away our old financial and economic beliefs?

A: In the twenty-first century, we don't trade anymore; the notion of "means of production" has become a fallacy. The market has been replaced by open interaction, and now, more than ever, people acquire and own the means to engage, participate, or get involved in an organization. In light of this new paradigm, it is an abomination that moneyers still get the lion's share of an enterprise's surplus. In Cast Away: For These Reasons, I make the case for a reexamination of the way in which we view and negotiate recompense. And this is where Ethosism comes into play.

Q: What is "Ethosism," and why do people need to understand this concept?

A: Ethosism is a term that I coined to reflect the individualization of open interactions that are occurring now in our daily lives. However, the world has yet to stop listening to capitalist pleasers and lumpen-intellectuals, and to accept this new paradigm as a new way of framing commerce. It's a true meritocracy system that could put 99 percent to the top while taking care of the 1 percent at the bottom. In my book, I go even further and say, "Let's get rid of economics all together; it is plagued with stupid cacophony. Why not start fresh with a quantum paradigm study of the way we transform, sell and buy, and, above all, distribute surplus."

Q: How can "Ethosism" shore us up against a corrupted money system?

A: A lot people have asked me the same question. Put aside that there is no fix to evil and keep in mind that, unlike ISIS, which will chop your hands off for stealing, this social economic revolution in my advised framework will take the power away from cigar-smoking capitalists. In doing so, it will detoxify the remnants of our financial culture.

Q: Where can we get your book and learn more about "Ethosism"?

A: Hold on for a minute! Cast Away: For These Reasons has just been out for couple of months, now. Even though I wrote all of my books around the same time, I decided to launch Cast Away first, because there are concepts and terminologies that need to be digested. The French edition of Cast Away, L'enfer c'est lui, is coming out in May 2015, and I think that a year is enough to build a platform for a new social economic injustice debate before releasing my second book. Ethosism is currently listed, ready for pre-order, and will be available on December 25, 2015.

Interviewed by Robert J.R. Graham.
February 1, 2015

Nova Harmonia

"From time immemorial, man has desired to comprehend the complexity of nature in terms of as few elementary concepts as possible."

—MOHAMMAD ABDUS SALAM

9

Tabula Rasa

"All men are endowed with the same qualities and the same faults, without distinction of color or anatomical form. The races are equal."

—JOSEPH AUGUSTE ANTÉNOR FIRMIN

THE PREMISE THAT ALL humans are equal based on the potential of ending another's life is a longstanding conventional-wisdom. We differ from each other by the valuation of one's dignity and rights depend on the way in which one acquires and owns their means of participation, engagement, or involvement in a public or private enterprise. The twenty-first century paradigm shift as long cease to be solely the object of anti-capitalists' phantasms. When are we going to get to next the batch of political economy concepts?

Brilliant thinkers argue that the abolition of capitalism is an impractical idea. Even in a part of the world where the free market mechanism is not very understood or deeply theorized, it is extensively embraced and applied. Lumpen-intellectuals set up scenarios for an ordinary mind to be disorientated. Every ordinary mortal feels like they have something else to say concerning distributive justice, for which the prevailing sermons have become standardized. The poor faith is imprudently based on presumptuous sentiments of knowledge and the benevolence of the elite, on the overflow of common sense, and on the ability to know reality with certainty, in academia. Distributive aerodynamic calibration meets the standard of zaniness and sustainability by fooling the human senses.

A pericardial window in humanity's patterns of thought suggests that the perversion of equality from an ideology into an old social concept is all the more dangerous when the defiance to social, commerce and trade, and political wrongs does not take the appropriate form of an ideological exodus attempt. There is a probable reason for the triple coincidence of wants and touch-ups: to reshuffle wealth distribution cards between the moneyers, the laboring class, and the politicians. The trial was not all about mathematics and cute graphs until recently. Tools of information manipulation are replacing neoclassical monotonous tunes in the social change mechanism.

Ordinary folks embark on messianic crusades as they are persuaded that the best way to attain their social, commerce and trade, and political utopia is through the capitalistic conventions of pain's merits. In some baffling pretexts, they deliberately discount the incoherence of provided facts and the value of one's means. Society is in a state of perpetual conflict not because of competition for limited resources. The captains of industry limit the access or the availability of resources and its alternatives to lessen conflicts that they control or benefit from. The unnatural state of the business cycle creates economic immense booms and catastrophic busts. Chants against injustices have become spoken word fumbling acts. The asylum run by the inmates, which is social inefficiency, doesn't pair up with humanity's aim at evading environmental Armageddon.

The ultimate expression of what human can do with what we pull out from prejudice is exceptional. The festivities of the powers of human reason reoriented social focal points towards ideologues who make the mass gobble up codes. Solons sought to yank the most primitive elements out of humanity's mundane existence. The classical political economists drew and redrew the frontiers of humanity's harmonious existence. They were locked in the battle between flimsy empirical and hazy inductive analysis. It was a matter of sheer ego. Intellectuals viewed poor people as cattle to be herded into clearly-marked cages. In the interaction between multiple ideologies, the one with the frostiest theorists established primacy over the others. One would hope that these social construct properties are nothing more than a phlegm of the past; an anomaly, rather than the norm.

Ending up where something is exhumed out of prejudice jumpstarts the process of moving away from the bad interpretation of oneself. From the assessment of slavery's varnish to the excavation of current global anxiety's cause, there is clear evidence that every society carries the same genetic disorder. The mere existence of Amish, Hasidic Jews, Madrassas, tribal war, racism, and despots could pose enough evidence that we as humans are still not better than brutes in the way we use our neurons. Those common-sense deterrents hold simpletons from the twenty-first center of gravity. How else do we reconcile the persistent global follies and pointless hostilities with pretexts for socioeconomic inequality and the denial of probable environmental cataclysm? We all have an inactive chromosome for a predisposition to virtue, and the natural tendency to opt for evil. Without the distinction of the amount of melamine or organic shape, we are all a fusion of aptitudes and flaws. Humans' quirky propensities guarantee constant paradigm shifts.

> "Hope is like a path in the countryside.
> Originally, there is nothing—but as people walk
> this way again and again, a path appears."
>
> —LU XUN

One could stare at a screen for hours and days, or caress a keyboard for weeks, before spitting out something worthy of consideration. There aren't many variations on that. My contradictions added to my idealism, which amplifies the difficulty in learning new emotions or interpreting facial expressions. Most of the time I felt lifeless, irrelevant even to myself. To engineer an alternative to capitalism, Erik Olin Wright's matrix has three steps: elaborating a precise diagnosis and critique of the world as it exists; envisioning viable alternatives; and understanding the obstacles, possibilities, and dilemmas of transformation. The second step prompts one to manufacture a truth. The third step aims merely to influence readers to pay greater respect to people who are making valid arguments against money-ers' "raison de vivre."

Wright's principles are carried far and wide by dissenters who sit on their feet. The picture of Karl Marx glaring at me, his cheeks flushing, appears to offer no clue in another direction. I was, naturally, annoyed, and made a pilgrimage to Highgate Cemetery in London. I was trying to piss on Herbert Spencer's grave while examining Marx's tombstone, when all made sense: "The philosophers have only interpreted the world in various ways. The point, however, is to change it". Some people hear their inner voices with great clearness. I kept hearing George Bernard Shaw mumbling: "The single biggest problem in communication is the illusion that it has taken place" in my ears. It was like he was telling me that just because his voice was in my head, I should not assume that other people can hear it.

Albert Einstein died leaving on his desk an unfinished manuscript on the unified field theory. There was another grand chase, to create a world free of poverty; and that, for some, is just a thrill or, for most, is frankly foolish. The abolition of slavery was not long ago an impossible and impractical idea. Not respecting sanctimony is rarely convenient. Naïve souls who attempted to make social realities matter from within prevailing social and political systems ended up dead or morphed into an added feature of the crusher. Since the essence of existence influences more than the future of an individual, escape routes can only be found in one's desire. Social justice's aura, indispensable to separatist cults, is faltering on distributive justice awareness and relevance. Change does not depend anymore on distributive justice. Sages anticipate a bourgeoning attitude shift, from not working for people to working with people. Moneyers are hurrying to make a fresh, viable condition for self-enslavement. With the help of past practice curators, they have tricked the public into believing that productivity is the only option to keep the global socioeconomic boat afloat. Is it a choice between prospects or gambles? This scenario obviates the nature of being human and highlights economists' hallucinations. Our obsession with how to adapt is moving humankind steadily into the dark abyss.

Cooperative and self-sustaining computer connections around the world are slowly replacing formal education by offering the oldest tradable currency known in history, knowledge, in despicable quantity. The educational models today are increasingly being compressed into plots guiding students to acquire knowledge on their own. To survive the various global destructive vortexes, individuals have to continually stretch and add speed to their savoir by conjoining formal education, real-life experience, and hot-off-the-internet pieces of evidence. Information technology has yet to bombard us harmoniously with disposable noises, alibis, and statistics. The vast sea of skewed information and partial evidence disrupts the slight causality between information and wisdom. The journey from interpretation to inspiration to make information a piece of knowledge is not smooth, either.

> "When a great moment knocks on the door of your life,
> it is often no louder than the beating of your heart,
> and it is very easy to miss it."
> —BORIS LEONIDOVICH PASTERNAK

All human beings have a talent for picking up the vibration of events. Despots are frightened by it. Radicals tend to be overwhelmed by it. Moneyers want to profit from it. The rest do not know what to with it. It is a weird and weary place to be, to lose control of your life, but not your will. The ability to socialize and to learn how to socialize can be autotomized without losing the human factor. For academics, a mistake is not a pretext for leaving nature take its course; it is an opportunity to conjure up another Machiavellian scheme. The trimming down of what is to be human into prudence or solidarity is the root of all evil, in economics. One clique has portrayed human beings as cold, calculating machines pursuing prudence. They have reinforced a moneyer's view of the betterment of society. The other group focuses on imposing a sense of cohesion, as they believe that human solidarity is the only way to curb injustice. They have reworked Marx's shenanigans to deem acceptable the twenty-first century world. Minds which are not filled with economics lexicons easily grasp the confusion and meaninglessness arising from current diabolic arguments. Debating on the same old ideas is, frankly, pointless. We persistently keep trying to repair something that is burned for the sake of memories or laziness. Living beings have to inhale the scent around them, and awareness of their insomnia shades the validity of the accusations and my frustration.

The super rich's fortune is no longer attached to visible infrastructure. New social concepts' scarcity is organic when we let the old way of doing business creep in with the aim of distributing the loot appropriately among members of a given enterprise. We have been lucky so far; we have had couple global and regional heart attacks, but no stroke. Utopian ideals persist in the collective consciousness despite the absence of a robust intellectual foundation because people feel the paradigm shift deep in their guts. Time makes all observations constructed through human interaction with others fallible, and all theories revisable and perishable. Merchants of ideas should not just grumble and gesticulate their frustrations about this. The disenfranchised have been throwing a tantrum different way. There is a morbid satisfaction in patronizing our own by helping somebody who looks like us to climb on our backs and get a seat at the ogres' table. Socioeconomic avengers are making the idea of kissing the Boer and kissing the farmer seem to be an appealing option.

Capitalism gatekeepers and Shinigami phonies' sense of misery starts with "the study shows." The dissidents attest, with a certain degree of delusional hope, that the scheme is doomed to self-destruction. In these day and ages, anyone who believes that "Communism is the only way of human life" is probably a red army fugitive living in the dark age, and needs to come out. Activists bursting with the fuming desire to save the world are only good for parades. Their solutions intensify the margin of the tragedy and the difference between equality and probability. In a limited number of cantons, minute compared to the whole society, anger has been directed against only one aspect of capitalism or communism which affected that particular community at that specific time. None of the emissaries of the past are adequately equipped to address existing social glitches. Their recipes on the table lie in that fact that they come from times and places that doesn't exist anymore.

> "Living is not synonymous with merely having movement. It is moving in accordance with one's will . . . one could say that, with deeds, one begins to really live. Accordingly, when one moves by means of one's own will and this leads to the destruction of one's body, this is not a negation of life. It is an affirmation."

> —FUMIKO KANEKO

The Neoplatonism, the marabouts, the Spanish sages, and other aficionados and scholasticism from different periods have all based their recommendations on their apprehension of the bubble they dwelt in. Time bends and blends fate. Past waves of pensée clusters have sought to discover the central theme in everyday life sagas of people trying to satisfy their needs while other abuse them or make profit from their wants. The venial sin in social analyses was lack of lack of feeling, emotion, interest, and concern for the poor's physical and financial well-being. It conflated the privileged senseless measure of success and peasants' firm, religiously-based irrational convictions. The particular tendency to use clique beliefs and practices one is most familiar with as a reference for the norm impaired the meaning of merit in the allotment of privileges and burdens. Two notions gathered a consensus: that the laboring class was immature, and the racial scale of humanness went down from white (the humans) to blacks (the beasts). Intellectual recognition was a matter of judgment residing in the basilica or the aristocracy's sentiment. It was in the best interest of the intelligentsia to reinforce repulsive prejudices by spitting out hypotheses that pushed forward the frontiers of collective consciousness degradation. These were the days when protestors were slaughtered, rationalists burned on crosses, and humans owned humans.

The functional side of the planet thus doused left the twentieth century with a hefty dose of uncertainty about the future. The twenty-first century has the opportunity, the right excuse, and the means to redirect the locomotive pulling the social, commerce and trade, and political wagons onto the right track, in the right direction, and to the right destination. The visible pile of capitalism's casualties and anonymous offshore companies' vulnerabilities is setting differences in motion. To be born and grow up in a sea of pain is not enough anymore to make one believe that the whole world is nothing more than one big lonely city. A juristic shift in pleas is reshaping the orthodox concept of general improvement in living standards. The wretched way of articulating the right use of money is defusing the rich person's childish privileges. The world is not becoming less western; the periodic global variation is becoming less familiar to the western baron.

New wizard apprentices are demanding a broadband to the approach to economic teaching that would help them to constructively and compressively dissect phenomena their contemporary humans confront. Bitter controversy, developed over the validity of the benefit of western social policies, begin to draw challenges from the shittiest place on earth where these are implemented. The quest for enhancing the human experience has shifted gears. To a negligible degree, progress has been made in term of portraying commoners as greedy, lascivious, and deceitful in a lesser, pathetic way. Despite the fact that Western framework is the most inappropriate way to generalize behavioral undercurrents in a culturally vibrant world, the rest of social science relies cripplingly on it, for everything.

There is more going on than the snubbing of the cradle of thoughts as if reality is static or the argument is already won. Counting and arithmetic were kept for a long time as the bourgeoisie panache. Mathematics made its druids claim of fame. Humanity's spine's refurbishment, or blurring the line between individual liability and collective responsibility, is enormously more lucrative than finding failures, deflating ideologies, and preventing catastrophe. It is a daunting task to gauge the authenticity of hypocrisy in a field such as economics, theology, or politics when vanity and insatiability are in it in equal measure. Algorithms recreating human decision-making processes hold the ability to flip-flop on a more sophisticated level, which makes us human. The heterogeneity of discourse is useless when squabblers are looking for record adulation and applause from stalwart supporters of their tenets.

"An emotional debt is hard to square."

—ROBERT BECK

Despair is a psychedelic that doesn't induce euphoria, but imparts the feeling of what it means to be human. Disparity takes the ugliest shape, injustice pandemic, when it is fueled by wealth segregation and intellectual prejudice. The grouping of the 'have alls'; and the 'have nadas' is not done based on merit. One does not cross from one of these rigid blocks to another by adopting the other side's beliefs. As far as the rich are concerned, there's no issue as to whether the "kill or be killed" mentality is "right" or "wrong"; it is just "the law of nature." The poor believe this, too. We are all prisoners of idiotic and maladroit conventions. Our lives are of full of absurd self-assurance rituals. The defining factor in the housing market bubble in different places and times exposes the same stupid, hopeless optimism that fills the heads of rich and poor alike. Defying norms with arrogance involves denying ourselves nothing but the truth.

Our current over-appreciation of the Western hemisphere mischaracterized the triumph of right over wrong. The industrial revolution created a marked wedge between social classes, spewing mistrust, discord, and antagonism. Humans who chewed up other humans' hopes were not rare as hen's teeth. Productivity became synonymous with profit. For the European elite, it was a time of change; a time of great upheaval. For everyone else, it was time for comfy misery. Plantation owners sought the boys, men, and women solely based on their "talents". For the girls, their copulation subservience to their masters was an additional criterion. Fervent defenders of the right to act, speak, or think as being inherent to all human beings did not manumit their slaves. Their compromise reconciles liberty and the inevitability of evil in their colonies with the sphere of influence's expansion principle.

During the twentieth century, every social, commerce and trade, and political construct underwent more than rhinoplasties in a desperate effort to escape responsibility. For the right reasons, the capital is still defined as the part of wealth which was devoted to obtaining further wealth[1], as Alfred Marshall stated. The profane views of the labor class and hierarchical arrangements between commerce and trade actors remained the same. By lumping the poor together and poor countries in one pile, every side's propaganda machine was able to point out and sell stories of tragedy and triumph. The hoi polloi sleepwalked to a factory and performed a limited number of tasks. For their pathetic contribution, they received a minimal means of remaining in existence until their productivity mileage ran out,

---

1. Marshall, "Principles of economics 8th edn Macmillan.", 503.

after which they were sent home with a bouquet of flowers to wait for impendening death. This cycle made life a pointless charade.

> "The alchemists, in their search for gold, discovered
> many other things of greater value."
> —ARTHUR SCHOPENHAUER

In the olden days, minuscule and frail creatures were drugged and sequestrated to be transformed into killing machines. The boys who successfully completed the journey to becoming a man eagerly sought to prove their sadism in battle to move higher up the feudalism pyramid ranks. The ones who could not be converted into ogres were trained to be métiers to make and maintain items indispensable to their community. A fraction of this group went on to learn how to identify the properties of materials. The skilled and reputable self-employed artisans who safeguarded their particular trade traditions and rituals took countless tyros under their wings, from apprentice to journeyman. Only a number of them became master craftsmen. The King granted land to barons and vassals as he felt fit. This guild and knighthood system blueprint was not particular to a continent or a savage age.

Once moneyers mastered the art of illegitimate private gain, they began to dream of a perfect value-adding process. The transformation of the traditional class of farmers from an agrarian society into an industrial one squashed labor liberty and guillotined the labor class's ability to emancipate itself. After a more mature consideration of the industrial revolution which had emboldened the bourgeois in different places, moneyers arrived at the conclusion that they had merely misunderstood domination's meaning. Captains of industry retraced their steps, and at length succeeded in finding the key in one of the doorways where the people had at first appeared to know nothing about profit: academia. By externalizing the cost of training and building a workforce ready to be abused, moneyers opened formal education's floodgates. The devious philanthropy of moneyers who no longer believed in the salvation of their businesses through Christ opened another gate to the poor: higher learning. It led to the proliferation of science knowledge applications.

It is hard to break shackle of self-enslavement. The motivations of the industrialist moguls in democratizing education were not complex and varied. The poor sought security by learning a trade in order to join a business. For moneyers, the scheme ricocheted, fueled by a philosophical shift in the academic elite spirit of intellectualism which served as a trampoline of their factories' throughput. The longstanding division of labor slogans and the modern specialization speculation anthem have come to rationalize over-consumption without paying attention to the new quaint décor behind the scene. The impotence of the old standards is becoming profound, as our psychological cravings are becoming central to human existence.

Scholars mostly under appreciate the true essence of the paradigm shift; the direct consequence of the twentieth century social, commerce and trade, and political metamorphosis. A skill or a trade, or getting the aptitude to perform a specific set of tasks, is undoubtedly less significant than a means of developing the ability to act in diverse functions. What makes the twenty-first century a special time? The location and number of individuals who are acquiring and accruing superb means of participation, engagement, or involvement in contemporary discussions or enterprises have prompted creativity ecosystems all over the world. The egotistical way of covering the scent of ideological mortality is by devaluating startling present-day, large-scale socioeconomic paradoxes.

Spectrums of gadgets have heightened awareness. They are empowering learners to critically assess voices in their heads. Every day, folks have gained the right to conscience and the ability to code the future. In the western hemisphere, they are aware of both. The means of production has been demoted. Humans spend more time collectively sculpting, promoting, and fine-tuning foods and goods than farming or producing amenities.

A paradigm shift and genetic code rewrite threaten to give way to a different form of beings or natural selection. New devices have demonstrated that the human brain is much more sophisticated than we previously thought. Expanding from this neurophysiology breakthrough, the shockwaves of behavioral economists' verdicts should have been felt beyond academia. The melancholic social scientists' verdict is falling short in its importance by restricting the implication towards the bazaar and mind manipulation. Victorian guesses currently being used to justify why individuals do what they do are no longer adequate. It is challenging to explain to insiders the sins of their fathers.

Socioeconomic disparity has long degraded from organic to inorganic. The power of common sense should have sufficed to loosen capitalism's grip over our mindset, just as it did to socialism, communism, fascism, and anarchism. Collectively, the information superhighway did make us more eloquent and smarter-sounding. Humanity as a whole ultimately needs a mental shift and a moral reboot to break the psychological contract that has tethered humanity to old social, commerce and trade, and political arrangements for far too long. Humanity is waiting for a proper reason to revise the catalog of what would make the world a better place. I am providing two reasons. Ordinary mortals owning their means of engagement, participation, or involvement has become a global culture. Capital is in the twenty-first century that the means which are locked in to obtaining wealth, ergo, it worth repeating here that instead of the average number of labor hours, the quality of the means necessary in an enterprise to produce a commodity or provide a service establishes relative prices.

"There is no original truth, only original error."

—GASTON BACHELARD

The renewed sense of challenging the fundamental principle of loot sharing has been misguided. The most critical aspect of universal dissatisfaction in terms of social arrangements has mainly been snubbed in the ongoing debate over humans' primitive motives and obscene fantasies. Nihilism permeates the inner nature of few human beings. Thinkers of remarkable objectivity who made the world a scientific arena obsessively pushed and pulled logic from every angle. When individuals who were struck by an instinct for verity examined humans, they always found indignity. Their most extreme fluctuations gave us great concepts. They were aware how dangerous their ideas were, but they made their positions very clear. Despite their spiritual qualms about their answers, they stood their ground. Some hallucinations take a very long time before society and technology makes them into reality. In perhaps the most valuable byproduct of their exertion in declining divine surveys, common mortals became instrumental in propelling the emancipation of the working-class crusade.

On the surface, classical economics is facing the fading of public trust. Crypto currencies are crippling the public psyche and make us rethink the monetary circuit. The dismemberment of commerce and trade interplays is starting to be infused with socially inclusive approaches. The goal has become to help impoverished people attain the financial stability to stimulate the consumer cycle. Wealth redistribution on a national or international scale, just as tax hikes to punish ruthless, greedy creatures, is seen as the cures. Newfangled rationalizations of moneyers' influences and shoppers' impulses are steadily brewing. Alas; in reality, classical political economy pure thinking is still the main contributor to the inquiry into the world. The character of social and justice assumptions over the last century is the same under the globalization banner. Talking-tos most admired, on both sides, are simply noises. Without peeling off more layers, we would certainly misidentify the mechanization craze as mortal sin.

Revamped globalization schemes have weakened captains of industry's muscles and have pluralized oligarch's circles. Nonetheless, an investment in knowledge and the pain of keeping up with changes guaranties a higher return, but not the fair amount. Unlike the previous type of customers, shoppers' confidence varies often, and often contains fragments of more than one characteristic. The new humans react to the same thing very differently. Enterprise survival depends now on a consistency in figuring out step-by-step human and animal decision-making process.

An organization preference, shrewdness, and good judgment have to converge in order to break shoppers' indifference and to gain from the commerce and trade dynamic. Who is an entrepreneur, or is taking on greater than normal financial risks in an enterprise? Everybody who has tied their means of engagement, participation, or involvement into the scam. The conceptors (people who generate or conceive ideas or plans) and the moneyers have appropriated the title of entrepreneur for themselves. In doing so, they alone reap all of the benefits and rewards of what the conductors, the curators, and everyone else sows. The carafes of everybody's sweat and hard work's extract are labeled profit. Yet, nobody stands to correct the vile mistake of leaving out other conspirators of an enterprise's monetary and social surplus.

10

Alinéa

"To do something right it must be done twice.
The first time instructs the second."

—SIMÓN JOSÉ ANTONIO DE LA SANTÍSIMA
TRINIDAD DE BOLÍVAR Y PALACIOS

SINCE THE DAWN OF time, sellers consider romanticism, distress, context, and rage as strong factors in devising their traps. Hominids are always like an excited dog wagging its tail and waiting to chase after the next ball. Is there any humanoid left who does not care to have just now? Whether it is wanting something more, something new, something different, or perhaps even someone different, the glut of enticing goods, services, and machinery has given human beings pretexts and ways of being venal. Other than the number of alternatives for satisfying severe cravings, there is hardly anything new under the twenty-first century sun. Gimmicks are used continuously to make old farts taste, feel, sound, and smell new. Even when there is something new, people lovesick with the old made new can't tell that the new is actually new.

Every popular apologue has its dark reality. Ancient civilizations have left behind traces of hazing traditions and rituals which validate the universality of uncertainty's avoidance. The old cultural hubris and the industrialists' pious façades painted capitalism as the pinnacle of civilization and social perfection. English moneyers had zilch class. They were obsessed by creating transcendent explanations and answers to their communities' inequalities. Their versions of the commerce and trade Septuagint progressively decimated a certain emergent common sense around their time. They brutally shoved and locked poverty and injustice into a dark underground vault. Next, they begun to erect gorgeous edifices for middle-class self-enslavement. Even to say the word "self-enslavement" was to invite polemic.

On the humanization of the labor phase, something must have gone awry in the 80s for 1st Baron Keynes, CB FBA, to be thrown in the same league of false prophets as Karl Marx. Long-term recommendations for contemporaneous torments hardly incorporate paradigm shift constancy. The deployment of scientific breakthroughs rebooted men, women, and children's attention. Automation increased the ability to make more of things. Labor recompenses and working hours have not been juristically amended. But human beings are snatching others and are trading them like any other commodity, faster than ever before. Moneyers look at automation, which projects us in the future while holding everything else in the past. Great minds of the past who formulated solutions for socioeconomic wrongs now required more than one or two generations for a linear trend. We fell into Thomas Malthus's trap. Technology's taking off will continue to have awful consequences for labor for as long as it disassociates with means that it generates.

For the most part, the level of interdependence a society maintains among its members, and the extent to which people are forced to control their desires and impulses, are deemed factors irrelevant to socioeconomic injustice. At the same time, the assertion has prevailed that one particular religion is the only group to have silly codes of belief and old rituals. There is also a sense that coteries and theism constantly and instantly redefine only poor countries' sociocultural layers and loyalties. It justifies why common mortals tend to act in a more individualistic way over disputes. We do not join the collective enthusiasm unless it is to ghettoize social welfare. A predator has preferences. Wolves are major predators of rodents. Prey comes from the indifference prospective. Insect pests are preyed on by all kind of small birds. As far as humans go, the prey and predator roles are fluid. But we all fall prey to the fallacy of provincialism, implicitly making judgments based on the familiarity of what we are used to in our cluster.

Patching up ethical holes, as we have been doing, can no longer last like it used to. The incompatibility is due to the considerable gap between today's behaviors and the flourishing deviations and rules of recompense installed more than two centuries ago. A paradigm shift does not spontane-ously trigger the mindset's shift in the right direction. The world has yet to stop eavesdropping on capitalist pleasers, lumpen-intellectuals. We should instead be paying attention to the twenty-first century's cultural patterns, and crown the latest paradigm shift as the appropriate way of settling com-merce and trade wrangles. Materialists and relativists should not be the only ones to concede the changes in our existences. The idiocy of slum, ghetto, shacktown, rathole, and racial subcategories' frictions is the mere fact that poor communities hold relatively the same disgusting, musky smell of despair. The wealthy cheerers hold an idea of affirmation, that fortune is amassed only by agonizing the poor. The poor believe that their losses are directly caused by a new frail hand gaining access to the crumbs. As I said before, and I am going to scream out loud again: in reality, it does not need to be so.

Some perceptions are based on the collective views developed and maintained within a particular society, as opposed to existing naturally. People take them for implicit agreements among the members of a society to cooperate for social benefits. A social construct of a specific group im-posed on the rest of the society, or perceived as inherent, does nothing more than contribute to social volatility. The premise of prosperity has misplaced critical pieces in the grand pattern of human endeavor. The labor class has nothing to break the chains with, but prudence to relieve, and folly to cure. I shall admit that a global program to sterilize the children of anyone who reaches a particular wealth cap is not such a bad idea. A chance would be given to others to ride on the one-percenter wagon. More than that, it is time for an original social, commerce and trade, and political system. This ought to reflect the individualization of open interactions occurring now in our daily lives. Its skeleton should not be a pile of morality, ethics, and trustworthiness arguments. All humans, to some degree (or when it is favorable to them), subscribe to historic views on the evolution of human thought. To determine whether a new concept fits the twenty-first century, the measure of which is conflict resolution blocks using reason and reality, ought to be examined.

> "Competition is the law of the jungle,
> but cooperation is the law of civilization."
> —PYOTR ALEXEEVICH KROPOTKIN

Lumpen-intellectuals and moneyers have the infinite capacity to truncate the disenfranchised delusions and ludicrous misinterpretations of evidence regarding past civilizations into one dimension, which is then presented as vital to liberty and prosperity. Their fantasies do not spring out of tenuous social comfort, but, rather, conspiracies. A sage who comes with the sensitivity to actual human experiences or some sense of emotion gets placated even when the parallels between their rational and the real world are incredible. Instead, a caricature of unconscionable conducts at the bottom of the social pyramid are ultimately drawn out of their self-deprecating mosaic, and psychotic episodes induced by moneyers are placed on the forefront. The marginalized path from dogma's naïveté to disenchantment almost inevitably ensures rancor and embitterment towards those adjudicated, lower-ranking humans.

When we get in front of a mirror, we scale back the expression that is indeed naturally us. We practice what we think we ought to give. Universal indolence serves as a trampoline for the free-marketers' assertions of their triumphs over the financial crisis they caused. Neoclassical presumptions once again effortlessly resurrect the naïve sense of a new financial boom's longevity. The one world anthem is exhilarating, for cavaliers. The non-interventionism slogan, another one of the fruits of western moneyers and lumpen-intellectuals' collusion, is still able to tease out some of the appealing free market ideas about one's freedom. In reality, the unnecessary bond between residents of sophisticated and backward nations is widening commerce and trade's maturity gap between the two factions. The domestic battalions of unemployed readiness are tainted by the know-how disparity between wealthy and developing nations. Pathetic republics are seen, as their arrears wipe out, as a consolation prize. Tyrants are undergoing rhytidectomy procedures to fit in new realities. Labor's savviness is rearranging the moneyers and working poor's umbilical cords.

The substance of twenty-first century "conmerce" and trade reflections lack appropriate computing conventions to trigger the correct defiance to norms and conventions. The post-mortem claim is sealed in the western academia commerce and trade bubble. It has been abused in order to point out the social context of the crappy part of the hemisphere. Let's be sincere: e-commerce runs on r-commerce. The profit motive is not colorblind. It does care about religion and politics. The knowledge-based economy is getting framed as the story of competitiveness rather than a frantic contribution to social progress. The lure of recognition is overrulingly rational.

Humans are nothing more than symbols. It may readily be imagined that, after a long series of disillusionment, people begin to think in a modern way, which will improve their level of subsistence and comfort. The transactional relationship between master and the self-enslaved has, in turn, beautified the psychological degrading of everyone from the middle to the bottom of the human scale. The mockery of their labor is bloating the class of the working poor.

We potentially have enough wealth to pass around. But the world is fixated on substitutes for the right and wrong reasons, and is oblivious to the hidden cost of capitalism and the glaring naivety of communism. The scarcity hypothesis squeezes off wealth distribution's horrible mixtures while obscuring creativity. The endorsement of investment hocus-pocus and exciting financial voodoo proliferations are modern-day ruses to defer to Martians the responsibility of instilling reason in humankind. Ideology's recruitment and popular support relies more on psychologic coercion or weapons than on the coherence of opinions. Those who merely see humankind's new dreadful saga as something to approve or condemn have yet to go through the rigmarole of its evolution. As a species, we reign supreme over the earth, even with distinctive displays of a marked lack of wisdom. The age of electricity and phosphorescent beams feels removed from the story of our forefathers. Tolerance for social and political injustice in its natural shape and usage is deeply anchored in an obsession with singularity and the exceptionality pervading human history. The lasses-faire nature underwrites bestial phantasms.

> "Never have I dealt with anything more difficult than my own
> soul, which sometimes helps me and sometimes opposes me."

—ABU HAMID AL-GHAZALI

During the Cold War, there was an intense interest in the extensive experiments of brave youngsters on liberty under the auspices and with the approval of the leading countries, which added viewpoints from ideologically contaminated sources to foster bright ideas. The anti-communists, as well as their rivals, collectively recognized the duty imposed to upon them to permit all humans to benefit from the inherent right to a conscience, to some extent. Blocks leaders unleashed Beowulf's dragons on the supporters of the others. Moneyers and despots attempted to mechanize labor as much as possible to keep the poor man's disease from killing the rich man's child. What is perhaps most striking is that neoliberalists had to empty out their bag of tricks and hoary preconceptions in order to correct the asymmetric approach rationalizing the human experience. They did not do so. They become protagonists of Caesarism and the ineptitude that gnawed at national identities.

Typical researchers read history from their offices and extrapolate a certain truth. Others seek real human experiences by traveling, and share their discoveries with others. The latter makes a big difference in your value regarding your pocketbook, and on your ability to stir up controversy by adding different perspectives into the mix. On such a journey, you make friends who you will come to relate to more than family members or childhood friends, because you are bonded by values rather than an emotion. You run into personages and communities who are caught in the delusion of their pain and joy's uniqueness. You will be stunned by people swimming with their hands out as if they were drowning, while others who cannot swim are ready to dive into a bottomless sea. Because the same root of compassion is also the foundation for hate, everybody might need to love less, delegate less, French kiss less, and croon less in order to pay more attention; to do more good.

Pessimism curls when compassion no longer exists in the universal concept of being human. It has taken me a long time to once again lay down long prose about injustice and what to do about it. The conviction that this exercise would either be an irrelevant act or perceived as a selfish lament has paralyzed me. Movements advocating better wages and shorter working hours in the working poor fighting vanguard have created its struggle for emancipation. We constantly fall in love with flamboyant personalities of scholars whose ideas are stuck in the past, have only a slight nuance of the present, and project future probabilities with certainty. These reflect aspects of capitalism's identity rather than extraneous features of the exploitative device itself. We all need to come to terms with the idea that a disorder's permanence is due in part to the passive activism of the few washed away by the active passivism of the many. Moneyers are not capable of a compassionate act.

In the face of the general public's dilettantism in political economy and the panoply of luxury labor-saving gadgets, self-enslavement feels less demeaning and agonizing. Moneyers have persuaded a considerable portion of the masses, especially in developing nations, that a mixture of liberalized foreign trade and investment, relaxed state control, and investments in manufacturing machinery is a driving force behind the economic boom.

Squeezing the social embarrassments of the working poor like a lemon to extract the real question is seen as a vain task. Dictators and tycoons' follies de grandeur, which is not differentiable from moneyers' reckless greed, was undoubtedly essential for the sophistication of the working-class means of participation, engagement, or involvement in an enterprise. A class of the working poor is a historical necessity, to organically turn their bourgeoning new attitudes and desires into capitalism's gravediggers.

> "Truth is born into this world only with pangs and tribulations,
> and every fresh truth is received unwillingly."
>
> —ALFRED RUSSEL WALLACE

We have long decrypted why people strive for deliverance in really dark places, using fireworks. Socialism, communism, fascism, and anarchism's not-well-thought-out narratives of an insurgency resonated with twentieth-century adolescents. The total collapse of hope in Marxism's dialectical view of social transformation has reinvigorated religious zealotry, which is in the twenty-first century pushing over the cliff those snotnose kids searching for self-actualization in an alternative platform. Instead of trying to fit into the box of the known, we should have been crafting a more comprehensive and dynamic social, commerce and trade, and political worldview befitting the twenty-first century's reality. Alas, ego blurs creativity. The universality of the pursuit to become superhuman outdoes all other folly. The appetite for being context-free exacerbates information's obesity plague. Trapped between the past and future, we are on the outermost edge of figuring out the point of being human.

Cognitive manipulation and perception's reshaping have deluded the collective scientific expectation and made reality progressively irrelevant. Bands of zealous scholars have purged out the complexity of human behavior and uncertainty surrounding questions of financial injustice, preference and indifference, and the social safety net, just to name a few. Dogmatism narrows the approach of investigations and generates a sinkhole in teaching which empowers a sophisticated dishonesty of knowledge's claims. The nauseating features of our world are its obsessive faith in statistical significance to gauge the balance of goodwill's cost and benefits, and the consensus that central questions to human existence can only be answered numerically. In a way, there is merely a space for Wakaranai or Gembutsu.

Theories do not focus the mechanics of certain aspects of the world. Similarly, surveillance of an individual spirit while trying to satisfy the necessities of the body or conveniences of the mind offer different conclusions. The most fundamental of neoclassical economists' primal musts is the ability to daze and to sway the public with incoherent hypotheses. Attempts to clarify and determine the properties and consequences of moneyers' supremacy over other commerce and trade actors by focusing on concepts such as poverty and wealth distribution have only clouded the social injustice issue. Why do folks, in this day and age, perversely believe that socioeconomic injustices are a natural phenomenon of life?

Although money's accumulation and infrastructure are essential, productivity's increase is the key to spurring direct foreign investment and linking it with international markets. The danger of the neoclassical mindset lies in describing productivity as efficiency and then profit. Enterprise creativity spearheads productivity to the rate we come to get accustomed to. To forestall strife between traditional merchants' ambitions and customers' objectives, which had led to capitalism in the first place, innocence lent credence to unnatural social constructs. Uncompromising fanatics dispossessed the dissenters of their homes, forced some go into exile, and killed others on the pretext that they were cursed. For dogmatic adherents, exchanging blows and vitriol is better than pedagogic ostracism.

Neoclassical economics is the stem of the obtuse lumpen-intellectuals who persist in safeguarding the vortex of fallacies to keep the masses in a macabre sphere of confusion. A national body of law reflects the bias and distrust of its citizens during a specific period. Doing the right thing, from a utopian perspective, has yet to be done the right way, and for the right reasons. While some expressed popular anger at the free market, collectivist models were often used preemptively. Non-believers in the notion that hard science equates to mathematics do not get recognition, and are denied the right to render themselves useful to social actors. But it is not the fear of jeopardizing many things in the global culture which is keeping us from doing the right things. For the lack of proper reason and a way for changes, humanity stays with what is conventional for fallacies, even if they be hundreds of years old and have a stronger inner bond with us than the facts that walk by our side. At some point in the twentieth century, we abandoned the tradition of experimenting with new reality. I intend to renew it while keeping in mind that a moral ground is not enough to distill social, commerce and trade, and political injustices; or to bring down capitalism's longstanding racketeering schemes.

Commerce and trade have always been about taking advantage of essentials or caprices. Today, enterprises go above and beyond to make a want into a need by devising and adding functionality to products or services. The goal remains the same: monetary gain. Today, a business which merely functions as exploitation is becoming an outdated way of making money. Newfangled rationalizations of moneyers' influences and shopper impulses are steadily brewing. Enterprises interlock more than visions and passions for making the quick big buck. Concepts of disruptive ideas are riding the wave of artistic and scientific revelation created by technological shocks, to form perfect arcades. Higher-ups in an organization who use cat-o'-nine tails or play mind games to swell the monetary surplus are no longer considered to be socially, culturally, or morally cutting-edge. Everyone in an enterprise is an entrepreneur in their way. Production managers are orchestra conductors of individual means of engagement. In the service industry, enterprises leaders' functions curate converging individuals as a means of participating. Current commerce and trade stitch-ups of sellers and buyers' interplays are starting to be infused with social inclusiveness. It could potentially halt, right in time, the depreciation of the term 'collaboration.' In doing so, it will generate an appropriate social and political ecosystem for the twenty-first century.

> "In my opinion, we should search for a completely different flying
> machine, based on other flying principles."
> —HENRI MARIE COANDĂ

From birth, two big cats were carted from town to town. Just like their ancestors in the circus industry, they were beaten until the agony disrupted their primitive instincts. They were forced to eat, drink, sleep, defecate, and urinate in a teeny cage. The only relief from their imprisonment and their handlers' cruelties was during their performances in front of roaring crowds. They fell in love during this horrific circumstance. Soon after, they became the proud parents of twin cubs, a girl and a boy. Every night, the couple wondered how they could change their children's fate. The devoted parents saved every piece of meat they could. Before they barely had a chance to get to know their kids, they sent them away to circus boarding school. The cubs were expected not only to go to circus college, but to be admitted to a prestigious one on a massive scholarship. So, they did. When you are a first-generation college student, your hopes and dreams can scald your eyes. There was pressure. They had been raised in the belief that higher education would ultimately lead to more than the ability to roam around freely and have clean food and water. They put four years into acquiring and owning the means of participating, engaging, or being involved in a circus show.

After graduating with honors, they found the reality of post-university life to be bleak. The only option offered to them were jobs with less public humiliation and whippings compared to their illiterate parents. But the pay remained roughly the same. The circus went from jumping through some hoops of fire to more fascinating, sophisticated routines. This industry's recompense practices and injustices were still a disgrace to every species. We need alternatives to prevent more disappointed graduate lions and those who can not afford higher learning. Just as circus masters and handlers, they too deserve a lion's share.

This is mostly a collage of individual means for financial gains, as were pirate crews. During the "Golden Age of Piracy," everyone on a pirate's ship—murderers, thugs, and thieves—had their roles and duties appointed according to their knacks and knowledge. They had clever codes for splitting the gained assets and treasure between the crew in a fair manner. A pirate's income was tied to the loot the gang plundered. Bandits on the Bartholomew Roberts pirate ship were all aware that "The Captain and the Quartermaster shall each receive two shares of a prize, the Master Gunner and Boatswain, one and one-half shares, all other officers one and one quarter, and private gentlemen of fortune one share each."[1] Movements, mindsets, and attitudes that oppose capitalism should emphasize the procedures of rationalization instead of the actual consequences of its use for allocating enterprise monetary surplus.

Our penchant for procrastinating over a new attempt to break psychological contract has three layers. There are many ways of explaining or sculpting a socioeconomic story. The typical style is the neoliberal paradigm framework, which depicts how moneyers' foresight and labor muscles are combined to generate profit. This rational simplicity has an air of well-developed methodology. The fresh batches of truth-seekers face thorny theoretical issues mostly deriving from new social factors which tend to distort the difference between needs and wants. At the same time, the lumpen-intellectuals are aiding and abetting moneyers in fine-tuning the free-for-all fallacy, to the end all the powers of the poor. Attempts to impose a substitute to old social, commerce and trade, and political bonds

---

1. Tilly, *Trust and rule*, 80.

are always going to fall flat: our collective dreams have been monetized. We are more or less concerned about the cruel scheme of turning forced labor into a cash cow until we get shackled. Whoever indulges in collecting consciousness data as the principal method for demystifying human experiences or highlighting socioeconomic inequality nuances, runs the risk of a tense psychological block. The risk is worth the pain.

Proletarians' propaganda must touch upon on splitting the lot of philosophical underpinnings, which are of great importance to the rationalization of social, commerce and trade, and political injustices. After all, an enterprise is not like a business with crematory laborer aspirations. The ruses used to trap enthusiasm is continually changing throughout time. Hence force, we ought to continually review it as the chopping up of the monetary surplus. The Wealth of Nations, Adam Smith's magnum opus, is credited with moving the analytic bar higher than mercantilism solons. Let's entertain that lie. The book was an autopsy of the nature and causes of the wealth of individuals and nations during his time. The constant interplay of living creatures' minds and contextual factors have made know-how an alternative form of currency as we maneuver. It does not weight more or less than money in the metric used to evaluate one another.

> "An intentional object is given by a word or a phrase
> which gives a description under which."
> —GERTRUDE ELIZABETH MARGARET ANSCOMBE FBA

The wealth creation and distribution are the two old puzzles that keep restyling humanity morality. Wealth creation has become less of a nuisance; we demystified it during the various waves of the industrial and managerial revolution. Technological innovations activated by unquenchable greed have made blue-collar workers excessively productive and generated absurd fortunes. The expected paradox is that the socio-economic gap between the rich and the poor has widened enormously.

Before coming to grips with Ethosism, we need to admit that, for enterprises, the monetary and social surpluses have to be worth the risk that sales and marketing headaches pose. Every agent is engaged, participating, or involved in the manipulation of shoppers. The existence of the sacrosanct natural duality between laborers, landowners, and moneyers, or a nominal weighted recompense of any party, does not make any sense. They all ought to get a share of the manipulation gain or loss in a percentage base. There is also something else. There is a noticeable similarity between how a society, a nation, or an empire comes to be, to a diamond's formation process. A diamond requires many pressures, high temperatures, and other conditions in the Earth's mantle in order to crystallize. Then Earth poops it out through volcanic eruptions. Rough diamonds look like nothing more than any bizarre rock. The hypnotizing beauty of a diamond only emerges after a complicated process of hitting the rock on the right spots and angles.

What is money? Money slew the double coincidence of wants travesty. The density and the velocity of the twenty-first century's transactions have depleted money of the medium of exchange validity. Money in every arrangements and expressions has long ceased to be the bridge between commodities. It is nowadays the nominal valuation of the energy contribution to the humanity's needs or to the engineering of humans' wants. The appraisal is highly contingent of social biases and edifying fallacies.

These days, more than ever before, we have enterprises instead of commercial activities. A goal of an enterprise in a primitive to the most sophisticated form is to break shoppers' indifference by using passive to aggressive tactics more than providing a service and / or a product. The control of the monetary surplus by moneyers and the philosophical inadequacy of dominant distributive justice dogmas is a great concern of mine, and, I assume, to you, as well. Ethosism is based on the notion that through twenty-first century training and education, one acquires the physical and mental abilities of participation, engagement, or involvement in an enterprise which are as good as old money. Therefore, the recompense should reflect the paradigm shift of the wealth creation paradigm in the 21st century.

Here, I am going to repeat it: capital is that means which is devoted to obtaining more means through interaction with others. Labor is not the sole source of all surplus. Money is not, either. Henceforth, monetary surplus distribution ought to be from each according to his or her means, not to each according to his or her needs. Ethosism obliges the valuation of the means of engagement, participation or implication used or integrated in an enterprise to generate a social or monetary surplus.

In a social surplus, there is always a monetary piece. The valuation attaches a price to a service or product and when there is more than one actor involved in the mission to break the indifference of the shoppers, to award a percentage of the "loot" to each. Every form of recompense should be negotiated and there should be established a term of fixed percentage of the monetary surplus. However, demarcating lines should be drawn between industries in term of revenue, profit, and salary-seeking. An enterprise should be prohibited from engaging in activities in more than one commerce and trade ecosystem.

Compasses are only useful once you pick a stationary destination. Ethosism is a proper reason and mechanism for amending humanity's definition of making the world a better place. This operating system makes climbing in the billionaires' stratosphere harder, and at the same time, it makes social, commerce and trade, and political algorithms' symbioses sustainable. The hardest task for a restaurant is to convince people to come in and sit.

"Then I will speak to the ashes."
—SOJOURNER TRUTH

Most of our multidimensional processor, our brain, needs more than learning in order to be a threat to the illusion of awareness and the presumption of knowledge. Utopians collapse under the pressure of the endless editing, toning down, and partial reshaping needed to fabricate an amiable aura around their posters to gain attention. Seasoned dissenters are immunized against philosopher's block by impenitently dilating and humanizing the distinctiveness of their tones. While readjusting the unconsciousness part of the brain, one can easily be oblivious to living in an extraordinary period. The heliocentric view of commerce and trade, and how labor orbits the moneyer, is being rejected. The reductionists' change of heart on the state of our collective consciousness is not the admission of flaws in the human mind. Human beings are more than neurons reacting to nutrients. The impact of the internet is overblown. The ecosystem is finely tuned, to sustain our existence or suffocate us all. Moneyers have long understood our collective consciousness, such autonomy and complexity. It takes paying attention to pick up the waves signaling a paradigm shift.

Mad scientists are working on getting closer to the beam of light, the carbon silicon merger; part mechanical and part biological being. Would it be stagnation or boring to live without contemplating new thoughts or prospects, deterring us from being immortal? Alternatively, is the idea of perpetual sex or the immortal poor so great as to make immortality worth it? Science, technology, engineering, and mathematics have appeared to be vital cogs in the wheel of national as well as global prosperity. A popular principle is that fair procedures are the best guarantee for fair outcomes. Désolé, it is a myth. The Cuban irony demonstrates that despite a massive expenditure on education and infrastructure, the production of goods and services per unit of investment has remained steady, if not decreased. And a lot of people ignore that academia has not been able to gather a consensus about its definition, or articulate its uses. Economists would never admit their irrelevance to human progress and to the pursuit of socioeconomic equality.

Democracy is an archaic way to shop for ideas. When a society comes across a financial institution encounter, why do its political and social state worsen? It is seriatim of fumbles attributable to the limitations of the current mathematically contrived model and needs a wider lens; a more integrative approach. Nations ought to explore the unspoken social conflicts within their society: excavate their evils, re-integrate sympathy and reason, and look at the whole arc. Gauging anything without the admission of subjectivity is to conceal the measurement's malleability. A lack of depth and diversity are the scapegoats when uniformity is the order of the day. We ought to implement technological advancement in the market of ideas. How about we individually introduce a list of concerns which get bundled up as public aspirations and statically match them to candidates' pledges? This is an *ideacy*.

Art answers, science solves. Art or science's disregard for concrete realities poses an enormous danger to humanity and thoroughly deserves capital punishment or death. Economics is a lethal weapon abused by lumpen-intellectuals and political pundits to succor moneyers every time they are caught with their trousers down. There is much pressure on sages to sell capitalistic optimism. Economics as a branch of knowledge is doing humanity more harm than good. I am for the dismantlement of this outdated instrument and science. The onus to establish the conditions necessary for realizing this end cannot be passed on to academia. It would be like asking a lewd abbot to exorcise Lucifer. Their most famous recommendations are at the least perverse and preposterous. Ignaz Semmelweis's mistake was in trying to convince the culprits and medical providers instead of alerting victims and potential victims. He could not see himself confessing to or denouncing his brothers. Sojourner took her battle to the most hostile audiences. The dismantling of economics is worth more than a passing thought, since it is doing humanity more harm than good. We ought to replace it with a quantum refinement of economics. This task requires attention, since the form of human linear collaborations and manipulations and the beehive of misery are not straightforwardly justifiable by the outmoded models!!!

11

Diamond Perfect Cut

"In economic theory, the conclusions are sometimes less interesting
than the routes by which they are reached."

—PIERO SRAFFA

FOLLOWING THE LEAD OF Alfred Marshall, marginalists discarded the concept of utility and made up their hypotheses to rationalize the discrepancy or the reason why the price of diamonds is higher than that of water. English marginalist interpretations have since become an integral part of the mainstream's economic theory. Today, enterprise successes are fundamentally based on the participation or engagement of agents in the form of labor, concepts, or dough. Twenty-first century enterprise's creators and conductors ingenuously avoid the patent and start-up fund trap that made past geniuses go to the grave penniless. While it is difficult not to give credit to the profiteers and the Bolsheviks for pulling humanity from the dark ages, most observers can clearly recognize that their insatiability and guts have made the commerce and trade pie, the class of the working poor, criminal financial schemes, and social conflicts bigger.

A diamond is highly resistant to cutting unless you hit it at the right angle. In the old days, all gem cutters had was their instincts when scratching diamonds in the rough for their splendor. Unbeknownst to most of them, an exceptional optical symmetry within a diamond made by contrasting patterns, the scintillation, is necessary to produce a virtual balance of brilliance and dispersion. The correct combination of windows and mirrors turns a diamond from an unpretentious rock into the envy of the world. At the beginning of the 20th century, Marcel Tolkowsky figured out the specific number and arrangement of facets to construct the perfect system of interfaces and redirects: the ideal cut. There is no tribute given to the unwritten rule of Henry Morse, who got it right 40 years earlier. It was purely a hit-and-miss affair.

Graphs can summarize much information into one picture. In what I consider my magnum opus, Cast Away; for these reasons, I added graphs at the end of the book to convey essential information about the concept of Ethosism in less space. Many readers did not find my decision fair. I did not set up scenarios in order for readers to be disorientated. It all boils down to the parallel between price setting processes for goods and services and the secret of a diamond's brilliance. Capitalism is the combination of the best of windows and the worst of mirrors. Communism, socialism, and anarchism are the best combination of best mirrors and worst windows. Alternatives have held some combinations of every flaw, or an aggregation of confusions. And an authoritarian regime messes up its national commerce and trade scintillation.

"I start a picture and I finish it."
—JEAN-MICHEL BASQUIAT

Windows: Revenue-led enterprises consist of making an object, in its most simplistic form. These are activities that lead to an output. Revenue is derived from a just price or the cost of extracting and/or modifying one or more items with the active engagement of laborers, with either passive or active engagement of moneyers, and either the passive or active engagement of landowners to bring either passive or active ideas to life. All the engaged parties' recompense should be a percentage of the revenue.

Mirrors: Surplus-lead enterprises evolve around creative strategies for the selling of an object or service, or the maintenance or delivery of an object or service. A surplus is derived from a fluctuant market price (bouncing from the just price up to the natural price) of auctioning off one or more outputs without altering the substance with the active participation of laborers,

and with either passive or active participation of moneyers and either passive or active participation of landowners to meet either passive or active conductors' targets. All the participating parties' recompense should be a percentage of the surplus.

Scintillations: Public services and charities generate a fund (e.g., taxes) or donations (e.g., charity) directly from the active involvement of laborers and the passive or active participation of curators to bring one or more either passive or active societies' initiatives to life. The aim in the public sector is not to generate a surplus for any party involved in this enterprise, but rather for the general public's welfare programs. Hence, all the parties' involved recompense should be a fixed salary.

Antitrust laws should restrict enterprise activities to either (1) revenue-based, (2) profit-based, or (3) non-profit based. Whether you see me as an affront to the marginalists or testament to the political economy's classical pensées positives, vitality says more about you than it does about my sanity.

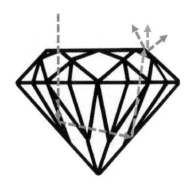

The Specter of Profit

"I ask no favors for my sex. I surrender not our claim to equality. All I ask of our brethren is, that they will take their feet from off our necks, and permit us to stand upright on that ground which God designed us to occupy."

—SARAH MOORE GRIMKÉ

Mama Vincent, Vincent, and I

Bibliography

Abraham, William. "The life and times of Anton Wilhelm Amo." *Transactions of the Historical Society of Ghana* 7 (1964): 60–81.

Acharya, Viral V., and Matthew Richardson. "Causes of the financial crisis." *Critical review* 21, no. 2–3 (2009): 195–210.

Adjibolosoo, Senyo. "The International Development Program of Activities: What are we Doing Wrong?" In *Ohio, A Paper presented at the October 2000 CBA Conference. www. ibuoffshoredominica. bafin. cbfa/Abjibolosoo_2000_Paper. pdf.* 2000.

Aiginger, Karl. *The current economic crisis: causes, cures and consequences.* No. 341. WIFO working papers, 2009.

Andersen, Chris, and Jean M. O'Brien. "All in the family." In *Sources and Methods in Indigenous Studies*, Routledge (2016): 133–82.

Ashton, Thomas Southcliffe. "The industrial revolution 1760-830." *OUP Catalogue*, 1997.

Bernasconi, Robert, and Tommy Lee Lott, eds. *The idea of race.* Hackett Publishing (2000): 17.

Boethius, Anicius Manlius Severinus. "The consolation of philosophy (VE Watts, Trans.)." (1969): 124.

Blaug, Mark, and Howard R. Vane. *Who's who in economics.* Edward Elgar Publishing, 2003.

Briggs, Asa. "The History of Retailing." *Bulletin of the Business Archives Council of Australia* 1, no. 9 (1961): 1–10.

Brown, Archie. *The rise and fall of communism.* Random House Digital, Inc., 2009.

Butler, Colin D. "Environmental change, injustice and sustainability." *Journal of Bioethical Inquiry* 5, no. 1 (2008): 11–19.

Castro, Daniel. *Another face of empire: Bartolomé de las Casas, indigenous rights, and ecclesiastical imperialism.* Duke University Press, 2007.

Choudhury, Masudul Alam. *Islamic economics and finance: An epistemological inquiry.* Emerald Group Publishing, 2011.

Clark, Gregory, Kevin H. O'Rourke, and Alan M. Taylor. "Made in America? The new world, the old, and the industrial revolution." *American Economic Review* 98, no. 2 (2008): 523–28.

Clark, G. Kitson. *The making of victorian England.* Routledge, 2013.

Clayton, James L. *The Global Debt Bomb.* Routledge, 2016.

Collins, Randall, and Sal Restivo. "Robber barons and politicians in mathematics: a conflict model of science." *Canadian Journal of Sociology/Cahiers canadiens de sociologie* (1983): 199–227.

Bibliography

Corwin, Edward S. "The Dred Scott Decision, in the Light of Contemporary Legal Doctrines." *The American Historical Review* 17, no. 1 (1911): 52–69.

Curran, Andrew S. *The anatomy of blackness: science and slavery in an age of Enlightenment.* JHU Press, 2011.

de Laffemas, Barthélemy. «Les discours d'une liberté generale et vie heureuse pour le bien du peuple.» *Guillaume Binet*, 1601.

Delcourt, Jacques. "Social Policy—Crisis or Mutation." In *Social Policy in Western Europe and the USA, 1950–80*, Palgrave Macmillan, London, 1985.

Dunn, Alyssa Hadley, and Morgan Zacheya-Jewel Faison. "The Shuttering of Educational Studies: Neoliberalism, the Political Spectacle, and Social Injustice at a" World Class" University." *Educational Foundations* 28 (2015): 9–30.

Elgie, Robert. "Exogenous political institutions? Constitutional choice in postindependence francophone sub-Saharan Africa." *Political Research Quarterly* 65, no. 4 (2012): 771–83.

Essid, M. Yassine. "Islamic economic thought." In *Pre-Classical Economic Thought*, Springer, Dordrecht (1987): 77–102.

Fiori, Giuseppe, and Tom Nairn. *Antonio Gramsci: Life of a revolutionary.* London: NLB, 1970.

Galbraith, James K. "Galbraith: A partisan appraisal." *John Kenneth Galbraith and the Future of Economics*, pp. 15–24. Palgrave Macmillan, London, 2005.

Gilpin, Robert, and Jean M. Gilpin. *Global political economy: Understanding the international economic order.* Princeton University Press, 2001.

Gintis, Herbert, and Samuel Bowles. "Structure and practice in the labor theory of value." *Review of Radical Political Economics* 12, no. 4 (1981): 1–26.

Goldthorpe, John. "The myth of education-based meritocracy." *New Economy* 10, no. 4 (2003): 234–39.

Goodman, Douglas J., and Mirelle Cohen. *Consumer culture: A reference handbook.* ABC-CLIO, 2004.

Groat, Lee A. "Funding for Gemological Research: Ideas and Case Studies." *Gems & Gemology* 42.3 (2006).

Heuman, Gad, and Trevor Burnard, eds. *The Routledge History of Slavery.* Routledge, 2010.

Heywood, Linda M. "Slavery and its transformation in the kingdom of Kongo: 1491–1800." *The Journal of African History* 50, no. 1 (2009): 1–22.

Hoover, Kevin D. "Econometrics and reality." *Maki, U.* (2002): 152–77.

Hume, David. "Of national characters." *The Philosophical Works of David Hume 3* (1985): 225.

Hunt, Emery K., and Jesse G. Schwartz. "critique of economic theory: selected readings." (1972).

Jameson, Fredric. "Third-world literature in the era of multinational capitalism." *Social text* 15 (1986): 65–88.

Joly, Vincent. ««Races guerrières» et masculinité en contexte colonial. Approche historiographique.» *Clio. Femmes, Genre, Histoire* 33 (2011): 139–56.

Kessner, Thomas. *Capital City: New York City and the Men Behind America's Rise to Economic Dominance, 1860–1900.* Simon and Schuster, 2003.

Khaldun, Ibn. *The Muqaddimah* (1377): 319–20.

Khan, Muhammad Akram, and Tony Watson. *Islamic economics and finance: a glossary.* Routledge, 2003.

Bibliography

Lall, Sanjaya. "Is 'dependence'a useful concept in analysing underdevelopment?" *World Development* 3, no. 11–12 (1975): 799–810.

Langlois, Richard N. "Rationality, institutions, and explanation." *Economics as a process: Essays in the new institutional economics. New York: Cambridge University Press* (1986): 225–55.

Leeming, David. *The Oxford companion to world mythology.* Oxford University Press, 2005.

Lelyveld, Joseph. *Great soul.* Vintage (2011): 74.

Lewis, Bernard. *Race and slavery in the Middle East: an historical enquiry.* Oxford University Press, USA, 1992.

Heywood, Linda M. "Slavery and its transformation in the kingdom of Kongo: 1491–1800." *The Journal of African History 50.1* (2009): 1–22.

Lucas, Micheal R. "Pricing decisions and the neoclassical theory of the firm." *Management Accounting Research* 14, no. 3 (2003): 201–17.

Machlup, Fritz. "Theories of the firm: marginalist, behavioral, managerial." *The American economic review* 57, no. 1 (1967): 1–33.

McAleer, Michael, Adrian R. Pagan, and Paul A. Volker. "What will take the con out of econometrics?" *The American Economic Review* 75, no. 3 (1985): 293–307.

Marshall, Alfred. "Principles of economics 8th edn Macmillan." (1920): 503.

Marshall, Alfred, and Arthur Cecil Pigou. *Memorials of Alfred Marshall;* Ed (1925): 427.

Morrar, Rabeh, Husam Arman, and Saeed Mousa. "The fourth industrial revolution (Industry 4.0): A social innovation perspective." *Technology Innovation Management Review* 7, no. 11 (2017): 12–20.

Olesen, Thomas. *Global injustice symbols and social movements.* Springer, 2015.

Palter, Robert. "Hume and prejudice." *Hume Studies* 21, no. 1 (1995): 3–23.

Peters, Michael, and James Marshall. "Education and empowerment: Postmodernism and the critique of humanism." *Postmodernism, Post-colonialism and Pedagogy* (1995): 3–36.

Quddus, Munir, and Salim Rashid. "The overuse of mathematics in economics: Nobel resistance." *Eastern Economic Journal* 20, no. 3 (1994): 251–65.

Restivo, Sal P., Jean Paul Van Bendegem, and Roland Fischer, eds. *Math worlds: Philosophical and social studies of mathematics and mathematics education.* SUNY Press, 1993.

Roberts, J. Timmons, and Bradley C. Parks. "Ecologically unequal exchange, ecological debt, and climate justice: The history and implications of three related ideas for a new social movement." *International Journal of Comparative Sociology* 50, no. 3–4 (2009): 385–409.

Rothbard, Murray N. "Classical Economics." *Books,* 1995.

Sandler, Todd, and Sandler Todd. *Economic concepts for the social sciences.* Cambridge University Press, 2001.

Schotter, Andrew. *Free market economics: A critical appraisal.* Macmillan International Higher Education, 2016.

Sekimonyo, Jo M. *Economic Jihad: Putting the Kibosh on Antiquated Social Axioms Defining Us.* Cambridge, MA: Venus Flytrap Press, 2014.

Sender, John. *Imperialism, pioneer of capitalism.* London: NLB, 1980.

Skousen, Mark. *The making of modern economics: the lives and ideas of great thinkers.* Routledge, 2015.

Strasser, Mark. "Mill on voluntary self-enslavement." *Philosophical Papers* 17, no. 3 (1988): 171–83.

Themelis, Spyros. "Education based meritocracy: towards a critique of post-war liberal democracy's most popular myth.", 2009.

Tilly, Charles. *Trust and rule*. Cambridge University Press (2005): 80.

Veblen, Thorstein B. "Boehm-Bawerk's Definition of Capital, and the Source of Wages." *The Quarterly Journal of Economics* 6, no. 2 (1892): 247–50.

Wade, Robert Hunter. "Is globalization reducing poverty and inequality?" *International journal of health services* 34, no. 3 (2004): 381–414.

Walster, Elaine, and G. William Walster. "Equity and social justice." *Journal of Social Issues*, 1975.

Wang, Susheng. *Math in economics*. World Scientific Publishing Company, 2015.

Webb, Stephen. *If the universe is teeming with aliens . . . where is everybody?: fifty solutions to the Fermi paradox and the problem of extraterrestrial life*. Springer Science & Business Media, 2002.

Westley, David. "African-language literature in English translation: An annotated bibliography." *Research in African Literatures* (1987): 499–509.

Young, George Malcolm. *Victorian England: Portrait of an age*. No. 12. Oxford University Press, 1960.

Zhang, Min, GuoDong Zhou, LingPeng Yang, and DongHong Ji. "Chinese word segmentation and named entity recognition based on a context-dependent mutual information independence model." In *Proceedings of the Fifth SIGHAN Workshop on Chinese Language Processing* (2006): 154–57.

Index

Adorno, Theodor Wiesengrund, xii, 19
Afer, Publius Terentius, xxxi
Africanization, 12
Al-Ali, Naji Salim H.,xiv, 33,
Al-Ghazali, Abu Hamid, xxiv, 121
Amo, Anton Wilhelm, x, 3, 8
Anarchism, 49, 114, 132
Anscombe, Gertrude, xxv, 127
Anti-immigrant policies, 5
Arab Spring, 22
Arkansas, 22
Arouet, François-Marie, 25
Arthashastra, 6
Atatürk, Mustafa Kemal, xii, 21
Aztecs, 11

Bachelard, Gaston, xxiii, 115
Bagdad, Iraq, 68
Bamba, Cheikh Ahmadou, xi, 12
Bangladesh, 31
Basquiat, Jean-Michel, xxvi, 132
Battuta Ibn, xx, 84
Beck, Robert, xxiii, 111
Bellamy, Edward, xxi, 95
Bello, Andrés, xix, 76
Bernays, Edward, 88
Biko, Steve, xxxi
Boas, Franz Uri, x, xxxi
Boëthius, Anicius Manlius, 13
Bolívar, Simón, xxiv, 117
Bolsheviks, 52, 131
Boucicaut, Aristide, 88
Butte, Montana, 68

Caesarism, 69, 122
Calderón, José Vasconcelos, xii, 16
Calvinism, 72
Capitalism, xvi, xix, xxix, 3, 5, 8, 22, 27, 30,
    31, 33–35, 39, 43, 47, 49, 51–54,
    59, 63, 64, 68–74, 76–81, 83, 84,
    92, 96, 98, 100, 101, 105, 107, 109,-
    111, 114, 117, 121- 124, 126, 132
Carlyle, Thomas, 15
Carnegie, Andrew, 21
Carver, George Washington, xviii, 69
Castro, Fidel, 52
Cateura, Paraguay, 7
Chae-ho, Shin, ix, xxvii
Chae-Ho, Shin, 37
Chinh, Trường, 120
Civil War, 22
Clarkson, Thomas, 8
Coandă, Henri Marie, xxv, 125
Communism, xvi, xxix, 3, 4, 8, 33, 53–55,
    58, 59, 96, 110, 114, 121, 123, 132
Conformism, 90
Coral reefs bleaching, 63
Cryptocurrency, 85

Dajabón River, 67
Dé Danann, Tuatha, 17
De Gouges, Olympe, xv, 50
De Laffemas, Barthélemy, 15, 16
De Mandeville, Bernard, 72, 92
De Secondat, Charles-Louis, 72
Derrida, Jacques, x, 6
Devi, Phoolan, xiv, 35
Diop, Cheikh Anta, 24, 26

Donham, Carolyn Bryant, 7
Du Bois, William Edward, xxxii
Dühring, Eugen Karl, 27
Dutschke, Rudi, 7

Edict of Nantes, 71
Egyptians, 11, 22
Einstein, Albert, 24, 108

Fair trade, 30, 31
Fanon, Frantz Omar, xv, 43
Fascism, 33, 49, 55, 114, 123
Feltrinelli, Giangiacomo, 7
Fénelon, François, 72
Feudalism, 50, 68, 72, 113
Firmin, Joseph, xxii, 105
Fodio, Shaihu Usman dan, 15
Ford, Henry, 22
France, 5, 72

Galbraith, John Kenneth, xvi, xxvii, 53
Gandhi, Mahatma, 25, 26
Garvey, Marcus M. Jr., xxxii
Graham, Robert J.R., 180
Gramsci, Antonio, 103
Grands Magasins Dufayel, 163
Great Chinese Famine, 130
Grimké, Sarah Moore, xxvi, 135
Gurdjieff, George Ivanovich, xix, 79

Hayek, Friedrich, 46
Herzen, Aleksandr Ivanovich, xx, 82
Hin-mah-too-yah-lat-kekt, Joseph, xvi, 55
Hooke, Robert, 8
Hua, Ong Boon, xvi, 54
Hume, David, 24, 82

Imperialism, 55, 60
Inclosure Act, 61
Industrial Revolution, 21, 22, 61, 78, 95,
    98, 112, 113,
Islamic economics, 4, 5, 33–35

Jacobins, 52
Japan, 24, 31
Jin, Qiu, xi, 10
Justi, Johann Heinrich, 72

Kaneko, Fumiko, xxiii, 110
Kant, Immanuel, 23, 24, 26
Karōshi, 31
Keynes, John Maynard, 3, 118
Khaldun, Ibn, 25, 26
Ki-chon, Cho, xvii, 65
Korzybski, Alfred Habdank S., xix
Kropotkin, Pyotr Alexeevich, xxiv, 119

Laissez-faire, 72, 73, 78
Lamarque, Jean Maximilien, xxxi
Lauck, Gerold, 88
Lewis, William Arthur, 3
Locke, John, 25
Loos, Adolf Franz, xiv, 41
Lorca, Federico del Sagrado, xiii, 31
Los Pistorelos, 23
Lumpen-intellectuals, 16, 23, 27, 29, 35,
    40, 69, 70, 72, 73, 75, 80, 83, 85,
    98, 101, 105, 119, 120, 124, 126,
    130
Lumumba, Patrice Emery, xviii, 67
Luxemburg, Rosa, xiii, 26

Magna Carta, 34
Malodor, 11
Malthus, Thomas, 118
Malverde, Jesus, 36
Mara Salvatrucha, 63
Marat, Jean-Paul, xviii, 71
Marechera, Dambudzo, xxi, 89
Marshall, Alfred, 3, 45, 112, 131
Marx, Karl, xxvii, 3, 54, 83, 107, 118
Marxism, xxix, 40, 123
McKinley, William, 21
Meidner, Rudolf Alfred, xxvii
Mercantilism, 17, 59, 72, 92, 94, 127
Mesopotamia, 11
Montesqieu, Baron. *See* De Secondat,
    Charles-Louis
Morgan, John Pierpont Sr., 21
Mühsam, Erich Kurt, xix, 77
Munefusa, Matsuo Chūemon, xvii, 61

Nationalism, 55
Nazism, 55
Negro Tom, xii, 23

Index

Neoplatonism, 110
Newton, Isaac, 8
Nkumbi, King Diogo I, 12
Noica, Constantin, x, 4
Nonconformists, xxxi, 23, 40
Nordau, Max Simon, xi, 14
North Korea, 5, 54

Operation Condor, 95
Oyo kingdom, 11

Paine, Thomas, 56
Pasternak, Boris Leonidovich, xxii, 108
Pérez, José Julián Martí, xxi, 93
Persians, 11
Pigou, Arthur Cecil, 45
Plato, 92
Potosi, Bolivia, 68

Radanites, 92
Ransome-Kuti, Funmilayo, xi, 8
Restavek, 36
Ricardo, David, 25
Ríos, Filiberto Ojeda, xx, 87
Rockefeller, John D., 72
Ruskin, John, 15

Salam, Mohammad Abdus, xxii, 103
Sankore University, 24
Sar, Saloth, xiii, 30
Savile Row, 111
Schopenhauer, Arthur, xxiii, 113
Schutzstaffel, 29
Selfridge, Harry Gordon, 88
Shaw, George Bernard, 107
She, Lao, xix, 80
Simon, Herbert Alexander, xx, 85
Simone, Nina, 7
Sisyphus, 61
Smith, Adam, 15, 16, 25, 72, 127
Socialism, xvi, xxix, 5, 8, 33, 54, 58, 83, 114, 123, 132

Socioeconomic inequality, 6, 99, 107, 127
Sojourner Truth, xxv, 129, 130
Sōseki, Natsume, xv, 47
Sputnik One, 53
Sraffa, Piero, xxv, 131
Stuart, James, 72
Szabó, Magda, xvii, 59

Tabula Rasa, xxiv, 94, 137
Talib, Ali ibn Abi, xviii, 74
Tazreen Fashions Factory, 31
Tirailleurs Indochinois, 63
Tirailleurs Senegalais, 130
Tolkowsky, Marcel, 132
Triangle Shirtwaist Factory, 31
Trotsky, Leon, 7
Two Cradle Theory, 24

Uno, Kozo, xxi, 91

Vachaknavi, Gargi, xiv, 39
Vanderbilt, Cornelius, 72
Vikings, 11
Vishnugupt, 54
Von Neumann–Morgenstern axioms, 95

Wallace, Alfred Russel, xxiv, 123
Wells, Ida B., xiii, 27
Willi, Alfred, 7
World War II, 29, 83
Wright, Erik Olin, 107
Wright, Richard Nathaniel, xvi, 57

Xun, Lu, xxii, 107

Yacob, Zera, xv, 45
Yevtushenko, Yevgeny, xxxi

Zhong Guo, 60, 69
Zhou, 11

CPSIA information can be obtained
at www.ICGtesting.com
Printed in the USA
LVHW020001230721
693426LV00012B/900